Problems in
Adult Retraining

Problems in Adult Retraining

EUNICE BELBIN
M.A., Ph.D.

and

R. MEREDITH BELBIN
M.A., Ph.D.

HEINEMANN : LONDON

William Heinemann Ltd
15 Queen St, Mayfair, London W1X 8BE

LONDON MELBOURNE TORONTO
JOHANNESBURG AUCKLAND

Printed in Great Britain by
Northumberland Press Ltd, Gateshead

Preface

During the course of its more formal research activities, the Industrial Training Research Unit has had many experiences of those human imponderables which can be so important to the outcome of adult training and of which sight is so easily lost in planning and administration. This has prompted a book, the greater part of which comprises case studies on a variety of themes including the recruitment of mature adults into training, the problems of slow learners and of those who start to learn at a relatively late age. Fear of large machines, of factory conditions, or of the need to learn maths; reactions to the images which companies create; identification with or a sense of dissociation from others who are in training; all these appear at various times to exercise a critical effect on the progress of those who present themselves for training.

Although we have addressed this book mainly to training officers, we believe it may also have implications for those in personnel work generally as well as for those who are involved in the non-industrial but allied field of adult education.

The Government report, *Training for the Future*, presages a substantial increase in the numbers of people in the middle years of life who will be given the opportunity to retrain. This book indicates some of the pitfalls that must be avoided, and outlines some of the approaches that can help to steer the endeavour towards a successful outcome.

EUNICE AND MEREDITH BELBIN

Industrial Training Research Unit
32 Trumpington Street
Cambridge

Acknowledgments

This is essentially a collective volume covering work by past and present staff of the Industrial Training Research Unit and others. Because we work as a team, much of the information collected by individual members is shared, and it is impossible to assign credit individually for each item reported. We are grateful to all of them for the material made available to us.

We should like, however, to acknowledge complete case histories contributed by Mr. J. W. Barber, formerly a part-time member of ITRU and now Senior Lecturer in Management Studies at Portsmouth Polytechnic; Mr. C. J. Middleton of GKN Screws and Fasteners Ltd.; Mr. J. Wilson, formerly of the Agricultural Division of I.C.I. Ltd. and now with the British Institute of Management; and Mr. J. Kirkby-Thomas who joined us for a few years after his retirement as Education Officer of the British Railways Board.

We are also grateful to current members of ITRU: to Michael Toye and Charles Smith, each for providing the substance of a case study; to Sylvia Downs whose wide experience over the past twelve years has enriched much of our material; to Dorothy Newsham whose contributions have comprised both help in writing some of the case histories and in travelling many miles to verify certain information collected; and to Trevor Warren for a large measure of editorial help.

Similarly, we are indebted to former members of the Unit —Dorothy Clarke, Tom McConalogue, Roger Mottram, John Neale, and Ella Warburton whose work also provided data to illustrate our comments.

The case histories could not have been compiled without the co-operation of very many industrial companies and other organizations which have given facilities for our research and allowed us to study and to talk to the personnel involved. In this connection, we should like to acknowledge our debt to the following:

Industrial Companies

John Barran Ltd.
British Leyland (Austin-Morris) Ltd.
British Timken, Division of the Timken Roller Bearing Co. Ltd.
The Carborundum Company Ltd.
Clarks Ltd.
Esso Petroleum Co. Ltd.
GKN Screws and Fasteners Ltd., Heath Street Division
D. Gurteen & Sons Ltd.
I.C.I. Ltd., Agricultural Division
Mac Fisheries Ltd.
Pasolds Ltd.
Procter and Gamble Ltd.
Scottish Agricultural Industries Ltd.
Selfridges Ltd.
Taylor and Penton Ltd. (The John Lewis Partnership)
Unilever Ltd.

Other Organizations

Aer Lingus
Beever County Primary School, Oldham (J. R. Kilgannon, Headmaster)
British Overseas Airways Corporation
British Rail
Cambridge Swimming Baths
Central Electricity Generating Board
Centre Universitaire de Co-opération Economique et Sociale (B. Schwartz, Director, now le Conseiller à

l'Education Permanente, Ministère de l'Education
Nationale)

Chertsey & Egham Institute of Further Education (R.
Brooks, Area Principal)

City and Guilds of London Institute

Garnett College

London Transport

National Coal Board

National Industrial Fuel Efficiency Service

Norwegian Ministry of Labour (Dr. Hans Arisholm,
Director General)

Post Office

Wool Employers Council (now Wool, Jute and Flax
Industry Training Board)

One of the companies whose experiences and procedures
we have quoted prefers not to be named. We respect their
wishes, leave them to identify themselves, and offer them also
our sincere thanks for allowing us to publish the case study.
From the list of organizations specifically quoted we are
especially indebted to Mr. J. Neale of London Transport,
both for the provision of so many facilities and for reading
the manuscript in draft.

This is essentially a book dealing with human problems,
and many individuals are referred to by name. In some cases,
the individuals concerned have wished to remain anonymous,
and out of respect for their wishes, a fictional name has been
adopted. Any resemblance to others of the same name is
coincidental. Whether we have been able to quote true names
or not, we are grateful to all those whose efforts at learning
have provided us—and, we hope, others—with so much useful information.

Some of these case histories use data which have formed
an integral part of ITRU's everyday research activities.
Others present information which was only peripheral to the
mainstream of that research. But none of the work would
have been possible without grant-aid. ITRU is fortunate in

that continuity of the research work which started on a small scale with aid from the Social Science Research Council and the Ford Foundation of the U.S.A. has now become possible on a much wider basis by a generous grant from the Department of Employment. We are fortunate too in the personalities associated with the co-ordination of this grant-aid—personalities who all too often remain unidentified in their Government Offices, but to whom we are truly grateful. In particular, we recognize the contribution made by Mr. P. W. Nickless, Secretary of the Central Training Council's Research Committee, whose personal interest has done so much to develop the link between official administration and research enthusiasts.

Finally, we should like to record our appreciation to Professor George Drew, Head of the Department of Psychology of University College London, for his administrative counsel.

We hope that by their and our efforts, the experiences described here may benefit the increasing numbers of adults offering themselves for training.

E.B.
R.M.B.

Contents

Introduction

This book is about the behaviour of people in training, and more especially about those who are being retrained for new jobs in the middle years of life. People react or fail to react, behave or misbehave, with, as it may seem to some, a bewildering lack of predictability. They may shrink from training after the most lavish preparation for their reception; they may dislike the training fare they are given (even though it was well received elsewhere); they may leave half-way through training; or they may react adversely to what they have been taught and fail to put it into practice. But for others the story is different. Under favourable conditions, training produces widespread benefits; not only are the requisite skills learned but a new spirit of goodwill, enthusiasm, and constructive effort permeates the whole organization.

Before we start our narrative we must say a few words about ourselves. ITRU (the Industrial Training Research Unit) is mainly engaged in the development of new training designs and principles and in the conduct of field experiments and demonstration projects in industry. So it is something of a departure for us to turn aside from our everyday business and to write about the more personal aspects of training and about those who may in the past have been considered too old to learn. We hope the following points will justify our choice of subject.

The first is a realization that the tradition of training in British industry has been largely shaped by experience gained in dealing with school-leavers. But since the passing of the Industrial Training Act (1964) the scope and scale of training has expanded prodigiously so that the subject now encom-

passes all age groups of the working population except for a
minority within sight of retirement. The importance of training for adult workers has received an added impetus from
the effects of mergers, rationalization, automation, and similar
developments that are bringing about major changes in the
structure of employment. With the decision of the Government to bring retraining further within the public orbit, adult
training seems likely to remain a major issue of the future.

The second reason underlying our choice of subject arises
from an awareness that the newly appointed training officer
has much useful material to read on training administration,
on the analysis of skills and on the techniques of training,
but that he very often lacks experience in coping with
individual and personal problems as they affect the system.
In seeking to meet this need we have collected a number of
real-life case studies, concentrating on those that carry a
measure of generality.

The third and final reason is internal and reflects our
historical development. In 1968, ITRU replaced the Research Unit into Problems of Industrial Retraining which
had obtained half of its financial support from the American
Ford Foundation's Aging Research Program and the other
half from the then Department of Scientific and Industrial
Research. This earlier research centred our attention on the
restricted population of middle-aged workers taking on new
jobs. Some part of our subject matter is due directly, therefore, to the support we have received in the past for work in
this area and our desire to place on record our experiences
gained during this period.

The selection of chapters and chapter titles cover some of
the major factors, which in our view, need to be taken into
account in the training of adults for new jobs. Each of these
chapters starts with an introduction which gives some indication of the subject matter of the case studies and the reason
for their inclusion. After the case studies themselves there
are 'Guides to Action', which set out remedies and strategies
for meeting the problems outlined.

The book begins with a chapter that may be justified as differing somewhat from those that follow. Here we have set out to examine the disappointing response of many middle-aged recruits to the enticements of training. Non-events are difficult to study, so that our treatment of this material has had to be adapted accordingly. Yet as age increases, the 'might have beens' and those who are unwilling to move outside their own restricted field of experience become a growing body of people who increasingly demand the attention of those concerned with re-employment in later life.

The bulk of our book, however, is concerned with case studies in which the central figures—the trainees and the instructors—speak for themselves. We have not set out to prejudge what they have to say, nor to criticize, but to collate it and arrange it, grouping like with like so that recurring themes come together in the same chapter.

In Chapter 7 we have set out the lessons that emerge from these cases in the hope that their exposition will have some general value for those engaged in the teaching of occupational skills to mature adults. In Chapter 8 we assess briefly the prospects of extending the scale and scope of adult re-training in the light of proposed new Government measures and facilities.

1. Unused Potential

INTRODUCTION: WHY DON'T THEY APPLY?

Time, energy, and money are spent in interviewing. This expenditure is justified if unsuitable applicants can be identified and if the likely problems of those selected are recognized and subsequently acted upon by adjusting induction and training procedures to their needs. It is wasted if potentially good applicants are rejected or offers of employment are refused.

Companies usually learn a great deal about the people they engage, both during recruitment and in subsequent employment. They learn little, however, about those who apply but decline an offer of employment or are rejected. They learn nothing about others who are eligible for appointment but do not apply. There can only be conjecture on how those not appointed might have performed, and on how fundamental were the obstacles that stopped some from taking the job or even applying for it.

Mature and older adults are over-represented in that great body of the 'not appointed'. Statistics from every country which provides them show that older people take longer than younger applicants to find a new job. In Great Britain, the percentage of long-term unemployment increases with each successive age group from 20–24 onwards, and if the overall unemployment figures vary little with age up to 60, this is only because of a corresponding reduction in the amount of short-term unemployment that older workers experience.

Such workers have enjoyed a measure of protection against

having to change jobs, through 'seniority rights' and the 'last-in first-out' principle governing relationships between employers and trade unions. As a consequence, older workers come on to the labour market less often. The protection they enjoy implies acknowledgment of the greater problems they encounter in finding new work, once they have lost their jobs. But the mechanism of protection works imperfectly. Reluctance to move away from the familiar work environment reduces the worker's competence to cope with a variety of work demands. A 'one-job' worker soon becomes typed and he appears an unpromising candidate for a new job. Protection erodes his employability, without offering him real security. He is safe during mild contractions of the market and from the effects of the pruning of labour when companies introduce labour-saving devices, but he is still subject to the shake-out which throws him mercilessly on to the labour market when whole units have to be closed down. Then his long-standing service may count for little and his prospects for obtaining such jobs as are available will depend on his general acceptability, the range of skills he has acquired, and an estimation of his capacity to benefit from training.

Employers do not usually peer very much beyond people's personal work history. It is not surprising, therefore, that the behaviour of people in 'categories' begins to correspond with the stereotypes in general circulation. Where some groups consider they are not very acceptable to employers, they are only too ready to retreat. As Wilcock and Franke* have shown in a study in the U.S.A., older unemployed workers, receiving more rebuffs, are easily discouraged and, in due course, become reluctant to search for jobs, to pursue an application, or to attend for an interview in a new firm.

The problems are common to both men and women, but in the case of women, the willingness to apply for jobs has a special importance for their employment. Whether they can be lured from the alternative of a domestic existence depends

* Wilcock, R. C. and Franke, W. H. *Unwanted Workers*. London: Free Press of Glencoe, 1963.

on a host of factors, cultural and economic. The consequential employment pattern is one of complexity and variation. According to the 1966 Census, 56 per cent of the women in Burnley were at work but only 23.5 per cent of those in Port Talbot. One estimate suggests that if the participation rate of women in the low participation areas could be raised in a boom period to the national average of 40–45 per cent, some two million workers would be added to the labour force.

How do middle-aged women view going out to work, what inducements attract them, and how does their limited or out-of-date experience affect them in seeking jobs requiring training? These become crucial questions.

This chapter is focused on the factors that influence the entry into employment of mature adults. ITRU examined the case histories of several firms which decided to recruit the over-30s for jobs requiring training. In some, only a few applicants (and in some, none) got as far as actually starting on the job. In other cases, recruitment was entirely successful. Something about the experience of these organizations transmits the message that many an employing body is not yet geared to attracting, receiving and placing the mature adult applicant.

1. ELUSIVE STARTERS

Forming an older worker night shift

In the early 1950s, The Carborundum Co. Ltd, acting very much in advance of current practice at that time, decided to recruit for training men in their 40s and 50s. The (then) *Manchester Guardian* carried their advertisement under a box number:

'It is frequently stated that men over 40 years of age have difficulty in finding employment. We are considering the formation of a permanent night shift employing men between 40 and 60 years of age, if applications received are sufficient to justify the experiment.'

The company was deluged with replies, over 500 men applying for the thirty jobs available, though some applications came from men well over 60, and others from men in their 20s and 30s.

The management selected ninety for interview and they were invited to attend at the personnel office, 'when the type of work available can be explained to you and your suitability determined.' All were men aged between 45 and 55 and lived in the various outlying suburbs of the town within easy access of the company and on a good bus route. There seemed little in the letter to deter the applicants, unless it was a blow to their self-esteem to be reminded that their 'suitability' was subject to the opinion of the company. Yet of the ninety men, only thirty arrived for interview, and only one of the others supplied a reason for not attending.

At the interview, it was explained that the work was to be in a newly erected plant dealing with machinery for grading and cleansing of the product. It necessitated some intermittent handling of weights up to 30 lb (14 kg), and the stencilling and painting of kegs indicating the type of product. Fairly low demands were made on skill. After a period of four to six weeks, a trainee should have been able to operate the machine sufficiently well to earn a piece work bonus and as his knowledge and skill increased, so would his weekly earnings. It was the company's intention to engage a number of older workers, train them for process work during the day, then transfer them to permanent night work, which over a period would absorb approximately thirty men in one section.

Of the thirty men who reported for interview, six refused the job, nine others were thought to be unsuitable for the work, and the remaining fifteen were engaged. Three failed to report for work and six months later only three of the remaining twelve were still employed by the company.

It was obvious from the letters that the great majority of the men were in earnest in their applications. Most were unemployed, others wanted to find indoor work with men nearer their own age, a few preferred the night work offered, and some wished to shed the responsibility of their present jobs. Many of them stated their willingness to adapt to *any* job.

This was a disappointing result to the company's appeal, especially as there had been no comparable experience when the firm had advertised for younger workers.

The years following this episode have seen a great growth in public and industrial consciousness of the problems of bringing mature adults into new employment. Older men should become increasingly aware of the possibilities of entering into new lines of work through the Occupational Guidance Service of the Department of Employment which was started in 1966. By 1970, the number of Government Training Centres had more than trebled to forty-five, and an earnings-related supplement had been made available in certain circumstances to men in the Centres to relieve financial strain during the training period. Even the tone of the 'situations vacant' column in the press had been modified. The shortage of trained labour, the influence of the Industrial Training Boards, and the greater awareness by employers of the variety of different teaching systems available for older learners, probably all contributed to the change of key. An upper age limit of 30–35 years in the 1960s was effectively replaced within ten years by one operating at 40–45 years. Before the larger scale unemployment of the early 1970s it was no longer a rare experience to read advertisements especially designed to attract the older inexperienced applicant because there was a much greater possibility that training could be arranged.

Experience shows, however, that, even where the climate is right, the recruitment of mature adults is beset with difficulties.

The new style advertisement

In June 1969, the following advertisement appeared in *The Times*:

'If you are over 50 you may have formed the impression
from advertisements that you are "past it" and that there
is no market for your skill and experience. In Selfridges
we know that many men and women, not merely over 50,
but over 60, are still physically and mentally fit and able
to do a worthwhile job. Many of our best staff could be
called "older workers" on this basis. If you can sell, pack,
drive, do clerical work, or have other skills and if you can
still do a full-time job despite being an "older worker",
then come and see us. We would like to have you with us.'

No clearer expressions of respect for maturity could have
been made by any firm. The offer did not suggest explicitly
that training would be arranged, but the range of skills asked
for was infinite. Such an announcement ought to have
appealed strongly to those older workers who are apprehensive about adjusting to a new job. ITRU approached Selfridges Ltd for information, and learned that there were only
seven applicants.

Earlier, during the spring of 1968, Unilever Ltd had
advertised in the London press for part-time copy typists to
work at their Blackfriars headquarters. The announcement
made no reference to age, but the company expected that the
hours would appeal to older women. Only five applications
were received. Two months later a similar advertisement
appeared, detailing a choice of the part-time hours which
would be acceptable, but the response was even more disappointing. None of the seven applicants who came forward
as a result of both advertisements was suitable.

The company then decided to arrange a refresher training
course for entry to their central typing service. This course
would attract back into industry married women whose
families were growing up—allegedly the only untapped
source of recruitment in an area of full employment. The
London suburban press carried the announcement specifically
addressed to women in the 35-50 age group, under the eye-
catching heading—'Your second chance of an interesting

career'. There were replies from thirty-two women, of whom fifteen were short-listed for interview. Ten were deemed suitable for engagement, subject to their performance in a typing test. All were judged as needing a longer course than had been planned if they were to reach an acceptable standard of competence. None was appointed. The candidates and the personnel office appeared stunned that their typing standard had been so low. Two or three months later, and with the co-operation of the firm, five of the women were approached to discuss with ITRU their applications and interview. Had the advertisement appealed in some mysterious way to the wrong people or was there more to it than that?

First impressions may be last impressions

Typical of the group was Mrs. Turner, aged 49, whose enthusiasm was roused by 'a second chance of a career'. 'The advertisement suggested that it was just the job I needed. Obviously the firm wasn't thinking exclusively of 18-year-olds. The pay was good ... I knew something about Unilever too: a friend of my daughter worked there, and they gave the roof for the Baptist Mission House where I worked in Africa. No, I haven't worked for twenty-three years, but I did take typing at night-school four years ago and took an R.S.A. examination. Since then I've been going to Maths and French classes.

'Then they sent me the application form. That annoyed my husband. He said: "What do they want to know all that for in a part-time job?" I was a bit more patient, although I must say it worried me. I was so desperately anxious to be interviewed, and an interview obviously depended on how well I filled in the form. They asked for interests, sports, etc. A housewife hasn't time for many outside interests. It looked as if I'd have to leave it blank. Then they asked for previous jobs and rate of pay. Mine all seemed so out of date. The pay of twenty years ago looked positively stupid.

'I felt one hurdle had been passed when I was called for

interview. I was amazed by the size of the building ... and I was absolutely over-awed by the reception lounge and so many little girls—all beautifully dressed—coming and going everywhere. Everything was so terribly "lush", it made me feel I must smarten up my own appearance. However, the person who interviewed me dispelled all my nervousness. No-one could have been nicer. Then I was taken by another little girl along the corridors to a classroom for a test. There was another applicant in the same room. Someone else gave me the typing test—it was very unnerving, as she watched me while I typed.* Another little girl gave me a spelling test.** I almost burst out laughing!

'If only I hadn't been taken around to different parts of the building and to different people! I might have done the typing better if I had been left on my own or if just the one interviewer had looked after me all the time and I could have done the test in a corner of her office. She was absolutely charming. Perhaps it's as well I didn't get the job. You don't realize how long it will take you to travel to work until you've tried it for the interview.'

Mrs. Turner was philosophic, 'I learned a lot from the experience and I shan't mind nearly so much next time when I try for another post nearer home.' (The company subsequently agreed that briefer application forms, less formal testing procedures and a more candidate-oriented approach would enable older applicants to do better justice to themselves in future. Their recruitment procedures were modified and the company successfully recruited and trained older women.)

How different was the situation for those who had to be screened by Mr. Cross. He was an employment officer acting regionally for a large national organization and recruiting people up to the age of 55 for training in semi-skilled work. The job was intrinsically appealing to many older men be-

---

* It was company policy only to take touch typists. It was necessary therefore to watch.

** This was Mrs. Turner's reaction. Tests were in fact conducted by the company's training department staff, all of whom were qualified teachers in their 20s.

cause it was not to be carried out within the confines of a factory or on a piece-work system. It afforded some scope for personal initiative and contact with people. Following one advertisement, fourteen applied, eight of whom were aged over 35, but only four (one over 35) were chosen. ITRU were allowed to sit in on the interviews. The low appointment rate was influenced by Mr. Cross's proclivity for using 'flap' in the interview as the basis of rejection. While he thumbed idly through the training manual or made mention of 'training school' or 'tests', he watched for alarmed facial expressions of the candidates. Any apparent anxiety and the applicant was summarily eliminated and left wondering no doubt whether he had any chance 'at his age'.

The age barrier

'If you're my age (51) employers don't want to know you,' said one man interviewed by ITRU from a sample of 206 who had been declared redundant in a range of industries. It expressed typically the feelings of 107 of them, all aged between 35 and 60, who hoped to get 'something better than labouring' and were prepared to train for new skills.

'If you haven't an appointment for interview, you can't get past the commissionaire on the gate. I've rung up to ask if there are vacancies. They've asked me a bit about what I've done, said they could probably fix me up and made a time for interview. When you get there, as soon as they ask "How old are you?", their interest dries up. They say "We'll write to you in a day or two" and that's the last you hear of it. Or they stop talking about what you've gone for and offer you a labouring job. I won't take labouring anywhere because once you do, you're stuck. They'll never move you up into anything else. They know you'll stay, even if the young men won't, because you can't get another job.'

'Some firms seem to forget that you've got to learn whenever you change your job. If I get another job as a fitter I shall have to learn *their* standards and what *they* consider is important.'

Those older adults who can gain no offer of employment beyond unskilled work see prejudice and fixed attitudes as the barrier, and actual capability as a minor issue. Is this image of industry which men reflect in their remarks justified? If not, how has it arisen and what is lacking in the art of public relations that it can persist?

2. SUCCESSFUL RECRUITING

Most adult applicants have to summon up a good deal of initiative to search out a new job. Unprotected by a social group and unfamiliar with the conditions or environment in which they think of seeking new work, they may be easily tempted to give up and many fail to progress along the road which is signposted 'form-filling', 'competitive interviews' or 'selection tests'.

Some managements are more sensitive than others to the fears of those they seek to recruit and set out to develop recruitment campaigns geared to the communities in which potential applicants live.

Familiar territory

Clarks Ltd, the shoemaking company of Street, Somerset, decided to review their methods of recruitment following a decreasing response to conventional advertisements. It was reasoned that to make a first visit to the factory during normal working hours is not very acceptable to most people. Those who are interested in changing their job find it difficult to present an adequate reason, either to themselves or their employers, for having time off work.

The housewife, on the other hand, would allege that she had to prepare meals for her husband and family at critical times of the day. But a more likely explanation of the house-wife's failure to apply was thought to be a fear of the unfamiliar and forbidding atmosphere of the factory office. Things might be different if the initial contact could be made in familiar surroundings: not in 'an interview' but by a 'chat' over a cup of tea. During such a meeting, the housewife would learn what might be involved in the job without committing herself in any way. She would also get to know a 'face' and this would mean something to her later in a more formal situation at the factory if she decided to apply.

Village pubs, chapel rooms, and other local gathering places were hired for a few such meetings, and dates and purpose of the 'chats' were publicized in the local press, on local transport and television and in shops and post offices. A day or two before each meeting, apprentices at the factory delivered leaflets to every house in the village. The response varied from village to village. About sixty women attended seven 'chats', and about half of those attending subsequently applied for employment. Most of the applicants were aged over 35 years. Thus by identifying a recruitment barrier, and taking appropriate action, the company obtained the additional employees required.

Simple forms, friendly interviews, sponsored induction

Most clothing firms fail to recruit middle-aged women as trainee machinists. Taylor and Penton Ltd—a branch of The John Lewis Partnership—attracted them into machining curtains, pelmets and drapes to order, through a careful assessment of recruitment problems. They recognized the crucial difficulties to be:

1. A fear of form-filling. A simple application form was used which called for no job history further back than eighteen months.
2. A fear of selection procedure. Care was taken to ensure that the first interviews were not conducted by anyone directly responsible for production lest he unnerve the applicant by asking technical questions. Candidates were

received by a woman executive, able to explain the job only in lay terms and who would put them at their ease. Only then were applicants introduced to the work room, the two chargehands and other women among whom they would be working. The section was a new one and the small nucleus of existing workers were middle-aged newcomers.

3. Post-appointment nerves—the fear of actually starting. The factory manager believed that a lot of women starting work for the first time or re-starting after a considerable break are bewildered and are shy about asking questions. Established employees are hesitant to 'interfere' but the isolation can be broken down if there is a formal relationship between the two at the outset. Each new starter was assigned to an established employee who acted as her sponsor. The sponsor was responsible for initiating the new starter into the general geography, climate and personalities of the factory and all matters excluding job instruction.

The firm's advertisement offering well paid work, with flexible hours and welcoming all age groups, was supported by the simultaneous distribution of 1,000 pamphlets by local Guides and Scouts. Both the advertisement and the pamphlet gave very full details of the job and conditions. Interviews were given to 100 applicants, and about thirty-five were appointed, very few of whom had been gainfully employed before. The youngest was 30 years of age and the average age of the group was 45. They started work a few-at-a-time and after a month's trial only one in ten proved unsuitable for machining and had to be transferred to other work in the factory.

These two case studies suggest that an approach to recruitment which is sympathetic to the feelings of the older potential employee can be very successful in attracting suitable applicants. Yet such an approach, backed by an effective training system, need not entail any loss in standards. Both companies expressed satisfaction with quality and output and succeeded in retaining in employment a high percentage of those recruited in their special campaigns.

GUIDE TO ACTION

Those in the middle and later years of working life find it much more difficult to gain new employment once they have lost their jobs. Employers who are prepared to recruit people in these age brackets have more choice and therefore a theoretically greater opportunity of making a suitable appointment. How can they make most use of this opportunity?

Attracting older candidates

The target population in a recruiting campaign should be allowed to infer that age is not a barrier to acceptance and training, and that maturity is welcomed. But direct appeals to 'older workers' should be avoided.

Adults are inclined to develop set expectations about the jobs for which they apply. The provision of fuller information about the requirements of the job at the time of advertising reduces the risks of persistent misconceptions and later disillusionment. The expected qualities and attitudes of suitable candidates are often as important as the details of pay and working conditions.

Campaigns that are based on neighbourhoods, social groups, and personal contacts can often be more effective than faceless appeals in newspaper advertisements.

Designing an Application Form

The application form must avoid questions that clearly have been designed with other groups of people in mind and which seem pointless and irrelevant to those who have to answer them. It is often better to design a new form for adult applicants rather than to make do with the standard form prepared for the recruitment of school leavers.

An application form suitable for adults can usefully include a section on spare-time interests and evening classes attended, the importance of which will be seen from consideration of trainees with the best prospects in home study courses (*see* page 142). Information about previous jobs should be confined to those held in recent years but can be supplemented by 'any other relevant experience'. Highly structured forms which involve long check lists, to which the applicant's significant contribution often seems negligible, should be avoided.

Interviewing

If the intention is to offer an appointee a full training, technical questions and discussion at the interview may be unhelpful and can be off-putting. A truer assessment of his ability to understand theoretical details contained in the training course could be based on the way he is able to explain and discuss the technical details of a job he already knows.

The applicants should be introduced to someone who will eventually be working with or supervising them.

If several applicants are invited for interview at about the same time, it is desirable that their ages should be mixed so that they do not regard themselves as a special category. Applicants can sometimes be interviewed together and this has the advantage that they can meet informally the people with whom they may train and work in the future.

Interviews should be held in a friendly environment. Unfamiliar surroundings can be daunting, some because they are dingy and depressing, others because they overpower with their elegance. Older adults often tend to opt for smaller firms. If recruitment is to a large organization, it may be useful to interview elsewhere until the applicant feels 'at home' with the personnel.

The applicants should always be shown the work situation —possibly at a second interview. This procedure enables anyone totally unfamiliar with, say, factory conditions, to amend, before they start, any false image they may have built up. It also helps them to feel personally involved in the decision that they could do the job if trained.

The training of adults for unfamiliar work should appear as a perfectly normal procedure in the firm.

When an adult applicant is rejected, it may assist him to know why, and firms are urged to give reasons whenever possible. If no explanation is given, he will conjecture—too old? insufficiently educated? too slow? or otherwise unsuitable? The opinion thus formed is likely to influence his future application for jobs, while the reason may well be specific to that vacancy.

Testing
Selection tests vary in how far they are appropriate or inappropriate to older recruits.* Professional advice should be sought if experience and expertise is lacking. In administration of tests already in use, allowance must be made for adults taking longer than young recruits to understand the instructions.

Analysing the drop-outs
The proportion of mature applicants who withdraw or fail to arrive may vary considerably. Ascertaining the reasons for non-arrival may help the reframing of future recruitment policy.

Induction
The provision of a 'sponsor' who creates a link between the learner and the management will help the newcomer to adjust to the factory environment. Telling the applicant about this facility at the interview will increase the chance of a newcomer starting.

* *See* Department of Employment Report of Working Party on Selection for Training (available through the National Lending Library for Science and Technology), 1971.

2. Anxiety in Older Learners

INTRODUCTION: MUST ANXIETY TENSIONS CAUSE FAILURE?

What proportion of the failures of mature adults in training is attributable to the effects of anxiety-tensions rather than to lack of learning ability?

There are some forms of anxiety commonly observed in industry that have a positive rather than a negative effect. A modicum of anxiety amongst employees, already trained, creates a sense of urgency, a niggling worry that an additional job needs to be done or that some standard task demands on occasion extra care and attention. Amongst trainees, a certain amount of anxiety may also be beneficial provided they are young: their attention is riveted on the task in hand and they are less distractable. But these facilitating effects are less in evidence with the older learner, for whom a fear of failure may too readily become a self-fulfilling prophesy.

Why should this anxiety of older trainees be disruptive rather than facilitating? It may simply be a matter of degree. Research by Professor Carl Eisdorfer in the United States has shown that if blood tests are taken before, during, and after learning sessions, the level of the free fatty acid content in the blood plasma (a sensitive measure of stress) differs according to age. Older people not only show greater stress, as measured in this way, during learning, but they remain under stress for a longer period afterwards. Eisdorfer has also shown that a rise in free fatty acid level can be related to poor learning performance.

In industry, there is a simpler means of measuring the

effects of 'new-boy' anxiety on learning performance. It is to give a learning task to recruits on their first day in training and then compare the results with those for a similar group of trainees who have been in the training school for some time. ITRU adopted this procedure experimentally on two occasions: first to comparable groups of middle-aged trainees in a Government Training Centre and, secondly, to two groups of managers on a polytechnic course. In both cases those who had been in training for some time learned significantly more than the newcomers. Provided the learning content is completely unrelated to the training course, as it was in these experiments, it can reasonably be assumed that any difference in performance is due to 'new-boy' difficulties. When a similar procedure was adopted with *young* trainees, however, the first day entrants were just as good at learning as those who had been there for some time.

While the learning of younger adults, unlike that of older adults, is barely affected by moderate degrees of stress, their performance may be disrupted at higher stress levels. In this connection there is some evidence from a study* of a very different population—parachutists. The Medical Research Council's Applied Psychology Unit at Cambridge found that performance on an unfamiliar radar tracking task just before a parachute jump was related to the amount of experience the men had of parachute jumping. Regular Army parachutists had the highest scores on the task and Territorial trainees the lowest. Inexperienced parachutists are relatively young but under high stress they may act like older trainees.

The situations in which older trainees are most at their ease occur where they are helped to transfer to another job through in-company retraining courses. In so doing they are less likely to inherit a traditional-type training programme built up over the years for a school-leaving population. A company usually does all it can to retain its established employees in the transition to new work, often tailoring the

* Hammerton, M. and Tickner, A. H. 'An investigation into the effects of stress upon skilled performance'. *Ergonomics*, **12**, 851–5, 1969.

training process to meet the demands of particular people. The potential trainee gains confidence from the knowledge that his employer believes in his ability to succeed in the new job and that redeployment contains an implicit, and sometimes quite explicit, guarantee against dismissal.

Where several of his workmates are being retrained together he is also buttressed against personal fears by the effects of group solidarity. Workers about to be trained for other work within a company have the advantage of knowing the environment and of being already acquainted with their fellow trainees and their instructors.

The first study in this chapter exemplifies all these favourable conditions. Why, then, were the retrainees anxious at all? Four labourers were selected for training as heading setters on screwmaking machines. Formerly, a man qualified as a heading setter after a five-year apprenticeship. However, a shorter and streamlined programme of training was introduced for the labourers. It was an uphill struggle, because the men were battling with themselves as much as with the content of the training.

The second study also refers to workers who became redundant—a group of twenty-two discharged from British Rail were taken on for training by a company manufacturing roller bearings. Their own idea was to take unskilled work, and it was only after persuasion by an enlightened management that they agreed to try for a job requiring training. While group solidarity gave them real support and encouragement and a sense of being 'all in it together', this did not allay their fears of being shown up individually as inferior to experienced operators.

Anxiety arising from embarrassment is illustrated by the third study, concerning adult trainee swimmers. Fears of appearing ridiculous, of being unable to learn a childish task or one considered beneath an adult level of intelligence can produce considerable tensions which can only be overcome by creating relaxed conditions that are conducive to learning.

Each of these case studies brings out some different aspect

of the way in which anxiety impinges on the adult's learning performance, while at the same time we can detect the pattern of events, sometimes fortuitous, that ultimately remove the barriers to progress.

1. FROM LABOURING TO TOOL-SETTING

It is some years now since the Heath Street Division of GKN Screws and Fasteners Ltd decided not only to train some older workers but to upgrade them in the process.

Training for the over-40s had been going on for a long time without anybody spotting that older trainees would have their own special problems. In spite of this, certain instructors had adapted their approach automatically, sometimes not knowing that they had done so.

Progressive instruction

One instructor, being firmly convinced of the older worker's resistance to change, adapted his method to provide a gradual but progressive introduction to new work. He would spend the first few days asking for the trainees' help in carrying out small tasks in the vicinity of new machines, showing them the machines in operation and endeavouring to capture their interest before placing any real training demand upon them. The value of this is illustrated by the experience of a second instructor who had begun to train a 63-year-old labourer to operate a new machine. Taken straight into training on the new machine, the labourer, overcome by an attack of nerves, started stuttering and trembling. The instructor was obliged to take him out of the working environment and into a lecture room where he succeeded in calming him by talking to him on general topics. This instructor was convinced that many older men whose anxieties were not so apparent, may have similarly suffered and never reported for duty on the second day. His 63-year-old trainee, however, with very careful handling, gradually gained confidence, learned to work the machine and retired after two further years of efficient work.

From incidents such as this the firm had gained insights into the training of older workers and a confidence that the problems could be overcome. At any rate, the firm was emboldened to try an unusual experiment by offering four unskilled workers, aged 50, 51, 55, and 57, skilled work as heading setters.

Due to the introduction of new machinery for cleaning, those who had been previously engaged in cleaning work were no longer needed. Their work had involved effort rather than skill, but they were on piece-work and their earnings had been high. If they had been transferred to similar work elsewhere, their pay would have dropped considerably owing to a re-valuation of the rates for the job. This would have been contrary to an agreement previously reached between the employers and the men. An attempt was therefore made to absorb them into work demanding higher skills and commanding earnings similar to those they had been receiving. Management had given an undertaking that during the process of redeployment, semi-skilled and skilled vacancies would be filled from the existing labour force wherever possible.

Unexpected fatigue

The work which each of these four men had been doing for a minimum of sixteen years was fairly heavy continuous labouring, unrelieved by lighter periods. It entailed collecting pans of processed materials from the machines, loading them on to a hand trolley and transporting them to the cleaning plant. Here they cleaned the material before taking it to the next operation stock area. The work involved much stooping and lifting, and as the collecting was done to a timed schedule, the men were continuously on the move.

The training started with some light sedentary work. But to the surprise of the training staff, the men who had struggled manfully under the arduous conditions of their old jobs now showed increasing signs of fatigue even with their lighter activities! They suffered from excessive tiredness, even in the basic stages of learning to read an ordinary rule. Could these four unpromising trainees, Donovan, Bates, Peak, and Thomas, really progress to the intricate jobs for which they were being prepared?

The new job

The jobs for which the men were to be trained was setting on heading machines. Heading is the process which produces the blank on which all subsequent operations in the manufacture of wood screws are performed. The machine cold-forges these blanks from metal wire. This wire is fed from a coil to the machine through a pair of rollers, then cut off to the required length and presented over the bore of a die. In a single-blow machine, one punch forces the metal into the die and simultaneously forms the blank to the required shape. In a two-blow machine, a moving slide presents alternately a roughing and then a finishing punch to form the blank.

The job of the heading setter is to set and operate these machines to provide the required blanks. To do this he must have a knowledge of the principles of the cold forging of metal, and how to adapt them to his work. He must be able to read simple blueprints and drawings, to use precise measuring instruments, and to obtain the necessary tools by reference to manufacturing instructions and tool standards. He is responsible for the quality of his work and must have a knowledge of quality specifications. He must know the faults that are likely to cause the blank to be scrapped, and how to rectify them. He must also be skilled at hand tool work. The job is intricate, has a high skill content and demands theoretical learning on the part of the setter.

What were the qualifications of the four trainees? Their education was low. Only Thomas had any previous experi-

ence on machines, and that was slight. The only other possible experience of relevance was Donovan's interest in clock
and watch repairing.

Armed with knowledge derived from the previous experience in the training of older workers, the Division was now
ready to start training. But although the instructors suspected
that they would have more problems than usual, they were
not quite prepared for the depth of those they encountered.

Donovan confessed that he spent sleepless nights worrying
over the work. He found the initial stages hard going. Yet
he was the man with watch and clock repair experience and
whom they least expected to be anxious; moreover he had
told the factory manager that he was confident of being able
to settle down in a training school and learn all he had to be
taught. He, too, was the only one of the four who thought he
wasn't too old to learn.

Peak's anxieties were expressed in another way. He was
afraid to approach the instructor for help—and he didn't
progress until the cause was ascertained. Notebooks would
help the men to remember what they learned, the instructor
thought, because it is always a problem for older people to
remember one thing while they are learning the next. But
what was not realized was that Peak couldn't spell. When he
was young, he had lost the power of speech as a result of
meningitis. He still couldn't pronounce some words. This
had left a lasting effect on his ability to spell, and not least
on his attitude to reading and writing. When his problems
were understood and treated with sympathy he started to
progress. In fact, he then went on to progress more quickly
than the other three. His instructor found him very methodical and meticulous in his attention to detail. He constantly
questioned every move and, in the instructor's opinion, his
refusal to rest content at any stage without satisfying himself
on each small point helped him to remember more quickly
than the others. What would have become of him if he hadn't
gained the understanding and help of his instructor over his
spelling problems?

Bates had a different behavioural problem. He did not proceed as smoothly as the other three older workers. After the initial few days settling in and the commencement of work on the machines, he seemed to have set up a barrier to learning. The instructor made every effort to overcome this but without any success, and felt that Bates was not making any attempt to try to learn. It was known that Bates was 'a bit awkward' and his reputation had preceded him into the training school, but whether this was unconsciously reflected in the instructor's attitude cannot be ascertained. The instructor attempted coaxing, leading, urging, and driving, and was in constant consultation with the senior and other instructors in an effort to teach him, but apparent lack of interest was obvious and no progress was being made. Bates himself asked to be returned to his old job and the matter was referred to his manager. At a joint meeting with the manager and Bates, the instructor declared he had his doubts about Bates being capable enough to succeed as a setter. The manager deprecated Bates' conduct in not trying to co-operate with his instructor, and persuaded him to make a renewed effort. At the instructor's request, he was placed under a different tutor.

For the purpose of this study, Bates was interviewed and proved, quite contrary to everyone's expectations, extremely co-operative. He said that he would give any help he could which would benefit the training of other older workers. In his opinion, the reason he had stopped trying was that, despite the fact that he was not progressing very fast, he *had* been doing his best, but he did not believe that the instructor thought it was his best, and had been worrying him by implying that he was *not* trying. This upset him so much, he said, that even when he tried, he made 'a mess of things'.

The instructor was also interviewed and while confessing that he had been 'constantly on top of him', justified this on the grounds that constant supervision was necessary—'as, in fact, it was shown to be if Bates was left to do a job on his own'. In the instructor's opinion, Bates' attempts had been so futile that it seemed he hadn't been paying attention.

These statements of instructor and trainee are compatible, but show that a working relationship had somehow not been established between them.

The new instructor also thought Bates needed constant supervision. His pattern of instruction was very little different from that of the previous instructor, except perhaps that he was more given to urging than driving. Perhaps the marked change in Bates' progress in training was largely due to the psychological benefit derived from changing instructors.

Fear of machines and the need for familiarization

All older trainees who passed through the training school had an initial fear of fast-moving machines. The four heading setters were no exception. So they were first encouraged to get the 'feel' of the machines by stopping and starting them and examining the workings. This approach proved successful, but in common with other trainees of similar age, they retained a great and sometimes almost undue respect for safety instructions. No older worker was known to disregard a safety instruction or wittingly commit an unsafe action during his time in the school. In particular, they worried about 'smashing the machinery' and it was not until much later in the course that they gained enough confidence to start a machine they had been 'setting-up' without first asking the instructor to make a check.

As one means of overcoming their fears the trainees were put in a group together, but as they progressed at different rates, other complications ensued. The final solution was to encourage them to mix with other trainees in the school who had reached the same stage in the training programme, and eventually the work situation provided the focal point for companionship rather than did the original social groupings. In due course, neither competition nor rivalry seemed to worry them. Each man was so fully occupied with his work and with making his own effort that he had little time to concern himself with the progress of the others.

Problems with note-taking

Every attempt was made to compensate for their long absence from formal schooling. Tuition started from basic detail and progressed in short stages. Notebooks have already been mentioned, but it was not only Peak with his spelling problems who found them difficult. The others did too, but for a different reason. The notebooks were just an added worry. The men found it unbelievably difficult to put their thoughts down in writing. The instructor persevered. First he gave them notes to take on items which they could easily remember anyway. Once they had sufficient practice in making notes, they found them an aid rather than an impediment to learning.

Perhaps their original reluctance to take notes was part of a general symptom of lack of confidence in venturing for themselves. Their old jobs as manual labourers had not required them to think. In the early stages of training, none would ever try to puzzle anything out for himself. They were always prepared to let someone else do the thinking for them. But heading setters had to make decisions to take account of special circumstances which could differ on every job, so the instructors had to try to overcome a basic reluctance to think independently. The approach was to ask the trainee what he would do, sometimes before being shown the job. The instructor would reverse roles and place himself in the position of the trainee. The answer 'I don't know' was not accepted. Gradually the men were coaxed into developing and acting on their own decisions.

Initially, all four men progressed very slowly. Much time was lost through being over-cautious. Many items had to be practised and reviewed time and time again before they were really committed to memory. Then, too, it was found that as the day wore on, extra mental effort was required and this used up their energies. Time was wasted in making silly mistakes as they became tired. One contributor to both tiredness and slow actions was poor vision. It was very difficult to

persuade three of the men to wear their prescribed spectacles.
They seemed to have a pride in the fact that they didn't have
to wear them at their age.

Even with glasses, it was found that the older worker was
at a disadvantage on very fine work. This was not thought
to be entirely due to sight; there was also a clumsiness and
uncertainty in handling small objects. Whether this was due
to a coarsening of the hands by years of labouring was not
known, but working with blanks under about $\frac{3}{16}$ in. (5 mm)
long and $\frac{1}{8}$ in. (3 mm) diameter took them inordinately long.

Four labourers qualify as setters

What were the final results of the course? They all passed as
qualified setters. Bates was the least successful, having been
tested on simple work only. Peak and Donovan were tested
on intermediate work and Thomas was tested on work which
qualified him as a setter competent to deal with any job. But
even Thomas said that his test performance was badly affected
by his nerves. He was much too anxious to make a success
of it, he said. They all described the test as a 'most harrowing
time' and felt their results might have been better had so
much not depended on the outcome.

What did the foreman on the shop floor think of the
trainees? Three of them were efficient and steady workers,
although on a restricted range of work. The fourth could
set most jobs, but tended to need the assistance of the leading
setter more often than expected of a fully competent man.

There had been no complaints from the rest of the setters
within the group that the older workers had in any way
reduced the group efficiency on which the weekly piecework
payments were calculated. Their timekeeping was good and
there was no absenteeism.

And what did the men themselves feel? Three of them
thought their health had improved, they had all put on
weight, and they felt they were making a useful contribution
to their groups. Each admitted that he occasionally required

the aid of the leading setter but '...so do the other setters'.

In all cases they felt that they had benefited from the training and felt grateful for the attention that had enabled them to be settled into skilled work and to achieve good performance figures. In their previous job, declining physical strength would have resulted in lower earnings. In their new job they were confident they would maintain their earnings until they retired.

The progress of the four labourers in training for skilled work did not go unnoticed, and, in a Lilliputian way, created quite a stir. In the year in which their training was completed, the President of the Screw, Nut, Bolt and Rivet Trade Society declared in his presidential address: 'That labourers aged 50 years and over are being successfully trained as skilled personnel is, in my opinion, without parallel in the history of industrial training'.

2. RELUCTANCE TO RETRAIN

The working population of Woodford Halse, a Northampton-shire village of 3,500 inhabitants, was once heavily dependent on the railways. When the railway depot there closed, twenty-two of the railwaymen declared redundant sought work at British Timken, Division of the Timken Roller Bearing Co. Ltd. Their ages ranged from 28 to 58. They had all spent their working lives as engine drivers, firemen, signalmen, shunters, goods guards, timekeepers or wheel tappers. Almost all of them had put themselves in line for general labouring jobs of which packer was the most sought after. Such positions would have entailed an appreciable drop in responsibility, especially for the engine drivers. However, the firm was urgently needing more shift inspectors, which led to the offer of new and interesting work but was contingent on the satisfactory completion of a three-week training course.

British Timken are manufacturers of a precision product. At their Daventry factory, all sizes of tapered roller bearings are made. Each bearing consists of tapered rollers held in a cage assembly, which is retained by the inner and outer components known as the cap and cone. The tapered rollers were made to a tolerance of one-hundred thousandth part of an inch, with rigid inspection procedures throughout manufacture, and the inspector was largely concerned with measurement and with measuring instruments.

The training consisted of a two week concentrated period of theoretical instruction followed by one week of practical exercises in the workshop. On completion of the training, each course member was expected to be able to read production schedules containing component drawings and to make subtractions or additions to given dimensions. To a limited extent, he also had to be capable of handling and understanding verniers, callipers and protractors, depth gauges, external and internal micrometers, slip gauges, dial indicators, and special purpose 'go and no-go' gauges. Simple arithmetical exercises were therefore part of the course. To qualify as an inspector, each had to achieve a 90 per cent pass in all aspects of the course.

Without exception, they had been apprehensive at the start. They felt that everything—their whole future—depended on how effectively they tackled this immediate training assignment. Morale was at its lowest two or three days after the start of the course.

As railwaymen, they had never before experienced factory conditions, and they found them more than a little frightening. Their main anxieties concerned noise and the discipline, indoor working, and the tempo of the production shop. They were also worried about the type of reaction that their presence might provoke among the experienced production operatives in the factory. How could men who had only recently come into the factory from outside be expected to inspect the work of skilled machinists? They visualized the arguments that might develop between themselves and the experienced operators, and they could see no easy road ahead.

Some of the redundant railwaymen were very conscious

that they had only ever had elementary school education. The thought of having to use decimal calculations in their job worried and discouraged them and slowed down their initial progress.

One man with forty-two years' railway service highlighted in particular the feelings experienced to some extent by all. He could not accept that he no longer worked for the railways. At every opportunity he would talk about his previous job, drawing others into the conversation. Firm control was therefore needed by the instructor to prevent the course members deviating from their training. To minimize these lapses he threatened the use of a 'railway box' into which each man would put a shilling whenever he mentioned the word 'railway'. This set off a good-natured rivalry, and the trainees were quick to take each other to task when the forbidden word was used.

The instructor noticed that each trainee felt similar misgivings, which were reinforced by a sense of group solidarity. Whenever fears, doubts and difficulties were uppermost, this group cohesion was even more noticeable. They were 'all in it together' and each individual member gave real support and encouragement to his workmates in meeting the training challenge.

One of the most important factors throughout the course appears to have been the particular role played by the instructor. He had exceptional background knowledge about the course members and was completely acceptable to them socially. In many senses he was a father figure. He too had previously worked as a railwayman, having left the railways and joined British Timken some years earlier because of ill health. He lived in the same village as the majority of the redundant railwaymen, and members of his own family were railwaymen. Some of the course members had visited his home before applying for work with British Timken, others went there for additional coaching in calculations after work. Discussion of course problems with him were often continued in the local village pub.

From the beginning of the course, the lessons were informal. Course members were given notebooks into which
they entered prepared notes. One of the group was then
selected to act as question-master while the instructor sat-in
and, where necessary, prompted the group. The effect was to
foster the competitive spirit among the course members without any apparent dominance by the instructor.

All the course members took their notebooks home and
carried on their studies during the evenings. Wives questioned
husbands about the many points of uncertainty. The notes had
been designed to form a broad foundation of knowledge.
They also served as a reminder of the detailed instruction
they had received in class. Once the basic points had been
memorized, teaching could concentrate on underlying knowledge. At the same time, through having learned the technical terms, they were able to participate much more freely
in questions and discussion.

Programmed instruction books were also used as an aid to
learning the many new names essential to the job. They
were of the linear type and allowed individual course
members to proceed at their own pace. Some members were
obviously at ease with them and were able to work through
the programme much more rapidly than others.

One of the slower learners was a man of 50 with over
twenty years' experience as an engine driver. In the middle of
the first week he had thrown down his programmed learning
text, declaring he would 'never be able to do it'. Progress was
resumed only after the instructor had taken him aside and
given him encouragement and personal instruction. At a
later interview the 'slow learner' took a surprising stance by
claiming that he had found programmed learning to be of
very great assistance! He was a noticeably fluent speaker and
had apparently been the informal leader and spokesman of
his group. Nevertheless, he confessed that during the first
week he vacillated between acute fear and sheer misery. At
the time he was convinced that he was the worst of the eight
members of his training group and he decided, therefore,

that he was not going to ask any questions because he felt that he would make a fool of himself. Towards the end of the first week he felt he had reached an all-time low and, in despair, had thrown down his programmed learning book.

'As a railway worker, I had grown up with the idea of never making a mistake. Making a mistake was the one thing you were always afraid might happen.'

This had made him slow and afraid of the training.

'I couldn't accept anything without checking and understanding it completely.

'I wanted to give up the course long before the end of the first week and had to keep telling myself that at some time I had to do a new job and that therefore I simply must stick out this course.

'Without the support of the instructor, I could never have carried on. This support was much more than the instruction I received. It was equally a matter of the amount of encouragement I was given. Particularly in the early stages, the instructor never attempted to rush the instruction. He left time for us all to discuss. And this had helped us to understand. In fact, the instructor went over some things time and time again.'

In answer to a question he replied:

'No, we were never bored. We were too anxious to be bored.

'I had been on the railways all my life and so had members of my family, yet I can honestly say that during my training at Timkens I sometimes completely forgot about the railways. All the same, I still find that being indoors can be very distracting. The noise still worries me. You start thinking and suddenly there is an almighty bang and you find you have forgotten what you had been thinking about.

'After the first week we had to take an exam. This

terrified me. However, when it came it wasn't too bad;
it consisted of a great number of simple arithmetical
and decimal questions. They were very simple problems.
I got them nearly all right. From then on I felt much easier
in my mind. I was able to settle down better to the training.
I even asked for my programmed learning book back. I
learned a great deal from it.

'Looking back on it now I can have a good laugh about
it all. Once you know the job you wonder why you were
so worried about it.'

This former train driver is now considered a very satisfactory inspector. In fact, all the men successfully completed
the course and in the eyes of the management fully justified
their selection. Many of them soon became competent enough
to undertake special inspection assignments in the factory.

Over a period of two years, only four of the original twenty-
two men left the firm. These four, of whom two were related,
constituted a 'carload' which travelled together to and from
work. They stayed together, too, in securing employment as
inspectors in another factory in a nearby town.

So railwaymen, who had seemed inseparably wedded to
their former industry, overcame their reluctance to enter
another and now, as inspectors, achieved a new solidarity and
stability.

3. OVERCOMING TENSION

Swimming is a leisure pursuit and ostensibly bears little relationship to an industrial activity. But the problems of
acquiring the skill of swimming are not dissimilar to the
problems of acquiring many industrial skills, especially those
of a manual character. A common feature is the finesse
required in the timing and co-ordination of physical movements, which, while deceptively easy to the onlooker, is capable of eluding many beginners.

The Central Council for Physical Education, disregarding
all the limitations which age supposedly imposes on indivi-

dual capacity in sport, has developed a campaign to encourage adults to learn to swim. In Cambridge, during one season, some sixty people between the ages of 20 and 70 attended special classes in the municipal swimming baths from which the public were excluded. These classes for adults have registered an 80 per cent success rate. 'Successes' are those who swim the width of the bath by the end of the course, while most of the 'failures' are early drop-outs.

This success rate with adults needs to be viewed against the general picture of the way in which age relates to natural aptitude. There seems to be ample evidence that those who make the most rapid strides in learning to swim are the very young children. As age progresses various types of identifiable problems come to the fore. Three swimming instructors in Cambridge described to a member of ITRU their experiences in teaching adults to swim. One said that in his view individuals begin to fear drowning from about the age of 7, and from then onwards the fear never seems to leave them. It appeared to be strongest in the late teens amongst individuals who were ashamed and embarrassed that they could not already swim. Later on, indifference and lack of self-confidence combined to produce an habitual rejection of any desire to learn except for those who had some special reason for doing so. Another instructor testified that the worst learners he had ever taught were sailors in the Royal Navy between the ages of 16 and 19. These, he presumed, were told that they must learn to swim to ensure advancement in the Service. The third instructor found university students to be very difficult to teach. They were over-conscious of a loss of 'adult' status at a period in their lives when they considered themselves mature. Some nursed an almost arrogant belief that being 'clever' they ought to manage quite easily a simple task like swimming.

Clearly these accounts suggested some connection between attitude and trainability. How was it then that many middle-aged adults should progress so well? Perhaps there was something both about the orientation of those who presented themselves in these special adult classes and about the way in which the classes were handled that compensated for some of the disadvantages associated with age. The experiences of two of the class members are revealing.

Forty-five year old Mrs. Parks and her husband ran a local post office and heard of the swimming course from one of their customers. Their main holiday interest was surfing, yet neither of them had learnt to swim as a child. Mrs. Parks explained that she had polio at the age of 7; she was under hospital treatment for the following few years and afterwards felt very self-conscious about her scars. This opportunity to learn to swim appealed to them immensely because 'as there were no spectators it didn't matter what shape or age one was or what sort of a fool one made of oneself'.

Every weekday their work started at 5.30 a.m. and continued until after their shop closed in the evening, yet Mrs. Parks and her husband attended the swimming class from 8.30 to 9.30 p.m. once a week during two seasons.

They found themselves in a group under one instructor with about six other learners who were also novices. There were numerous signs that group bonds were developing. Couples paired up for holidays and a class dinner was given for an instructor. The effect was to produce a characteristic outlook: 'when we are all in the same boat nobody seems to be embarrassed. In fact we enjoyed making fools of ourselves together. Nobody felt humiliated even when their efforts did not produce quick results'.

Mrs. Parks emphasized that learning to swim was not like learning to ride a bicycle. It came much more gradually. She knew what the movements should be, but the difficulty lay in achieving the right combination of movements at the right time. She needed to be very relaxed. The instructor, who gave his directions from the side of the bath, could see what she was doing correctly and where she was at fault, but being told what to do and being able to do it were two very different things. Being anxious to succeed, she thought, made them too ready to rush their strokes.

The instructor, for his part, defined three stages in the process: the first when no progress seems to be made at all, the second when it is possible to swim a few strokes, and the third when it is possible to swim longer distances depending mainly upon stamina and amount of practice. The second stage is the most critical. Delay in this phase or failure to graduate out of it is not because trainees cannot carry out the required movements or because they tire easily. Rather it is because they are so determined they become tense. When this happens they cease to breathe normally and they gulp. This in turn disrupts their relaxed posture which is a prerequisite for further progress. The most relaxed adult learners were almost certain to become swimmers provided they attended between three and six classes. Some were able to move through the water even on the second occasion.

Perhaps it is not just in the swimming baths that tension causes older learners to stiffen, to lose co-ordination, to flounder and to 'sink'. But where the effects are obvious it is easier to take some counter-action. In industrial training, learners may expire before their plight is realized.

Overcoming self-consciousness and tension can be the critical prerequisite to a burst of progress in learning.

GUIDE TO ACTION

Older adults are more prone to anxiety than younger people during training and take longer to re-establish their equilibrium. Disruptive anxiety may therefore cause their learning potential to be under-estimated. Management's resistance to the acceptance of older trainees is likely to harden unless it can be shown that their problems, whatever their underlying nature, can be successfully overcome. It is the responsibility of the training officer to design the course of training in such a way that the negative effects resulting from anxiety are removed so that the full potential of trainees can be developed.

Overcoming reluctance to train

The shunning of training and its counterpart, a tenacious attachment to jobs that are familiar (and usually low grade), are often linked with long separation from and a distaste for formal education. Misgivings may be further heightened by an awareness that those in training are mostly school leavers.

Adult trainees who are reluctant to make a start should be introduced to people of similar background who have been successful. Adult education and training should be dissociated from traditional school-room techniques. Modern methods are helpful in creating a new enthusiasm towards learning.

Where adult trainees have special problems, such as illiteracy or innumeracy, a pre-training course can be planned, but special care must be taken to present this as part of a total package rather than as an exceptional procedure directed at particular trainees.

Reducing tension amongst trainees

On many skills involving muscular control or high mental effort, little progress is likely to be made until trainees are thoroughly relaxed. Easy and less critical activities might be promoted until the moment is judged as being psychologically right for tackling the essential 'core' skill.

Meeting the adult's fear of mistakes

All older people prefer accuracy to speed. Many will have consolidated their skills in former jobs where they seldom, if ever, made mistakes. Pride in their sense of accuracy and reliability may inhibit them from making a response at all, since every trainee is error-prone. At stake is a loss of face. If a trainee is allowed—and, in fact, encouraged by the design of the training programme—to detect and correct his own errors in the early stages, he will be freed from the disillusionment and despair which often follow when his errors are later detected by those who supervise him.

Introduction to formidable machines

Most older men and women have had jobs in which there was an observable connection between human action and machine response. Modern machinery often makes for a more complex relationship between 'display' and 'control', and the uncertainties that this engenders increase the fears, if not the actual risks, of making mistakes on a large scale.

Trainees should be allowed initially to take on an ancillary job beside the machine, or to become generally familiar with its operations, before they are given machine responsibilities.

Disinhibiting the silent

Most older learners ask innumerable questions for they insist that they can only learn by understanding. There are the exceptions who say nothing. The silent student may be hesitant to expose his lack of knowledge, dreads losing his status, and is afraid of revealing to himself as well as to others that he has failed to grasp some essential point.

Where there is a risk that questions will not be forthcoming, they can be built into the training programme. There are several ways of doing this:

1. Provide questions which the trainees *have* to ask of the instructor in order to get to the next step.
2. Plan for instructors and trainees to reverse roles.
3. Allow trainees to work in pairs and to question each other's approach.

Removing the fear of failure

Whether real or threatened, withdrawal may be due to a fear of final examinations. These can often be replaced by continuous progress checks and assessments that can soon be accepted as part of daily routines and which are shared and discussed with the trainee. If a final examination is retained, preceding progress checks and assessment will do much to reduce the shock of its impact.

The possibility of ultimate failure should never be acknowledged. Trainees are there to learn and it is the instructor's job to help them do so. If unsuitable candidates are excluded at the outset (by appropriate selection procedures), confidence can be developed amongst all who start in training by building up real evidence that no one ever fails.

3. Starting Late

INTRODUCTION: SPECIAL APPROACHES FOR THE OLDER LEARNER

In the United Kingdom in September 1970, manual workers comprised 68 per cent of the employed but 83 per cent of the unemployed. Against a national unemployment rate of 2·6 per cent, the corresponding figure for male manual workers was 4·0 per cent, while unemployment amongst unskilled labour stood even higher at 8·4 per cent. The special plight of those at the lower end of the skill spectrum, which has been similarly indicated by studies in many other countries, emphasizes the potential role of retraining as a means of enabling workers to reach jobs which offer greater employment security. Yet even when the facilities are available, there are serious obstacles in the way, notably lack of aptitude and age.

For many skills there is a normal age range for learning. Above this age, most employers contend it becomes impossible or uneconomic to teach the skill. The age barrier might be as low as 32 for certain high-speed assembly jobs; for sewing machinists it is said to be around 25 to 30. What happens when an attempt is made to train people outside this range?

This chapter contains three studies in which the age of learning or relearning was so late as to be abnormal. Mrs. Chatton was a 50-year-old mother of a large family, entirely without industrial experience and with no specific aptitude. She was recruited into a training programme for high-speed sewing machinists for the express purpose of studying the difficulties of older learners. The nature of her struggles and her periodic bursts of progress, often followed by lapses, has contributed a good deal to ITRU's understanding of what needs to be done in the design of training methods for high speed reflex skills to fit them to the needs of the older learner.

Harry was another late starter. The middle 30s would not seem unduly late for most forms of learning except that his problem was illiteracy. Married with two children, he had made good progress as a maintenance engineer, cleverly finding ways of circumventing the need to read. Then he was faced with promotion and his shortcoming was glaringly exposed. The method of training is crucially important for the late learner, but motivation was also seen to play a vital role.

Our third case study concerns supervisors. They were mostly in the 40 to 55 age range and were failing to do their jobs effectively. They were acceptable to management until a major change in the production technology made plain the need for a different sort of supervisor. Is it impossible to change attitudes or style in middle age? When management says '...no longer on the right wavelength; never likely to make more than average charge-hand', is it really too late to adjust to another wavelength?

The late starter is of special interest for those concerned with training. There have been relatively few late starters, almost by definition. This is a field, therefore, in which knowledge is scanty yet becoming increasingly important when companies change the age composition of those they recruit. Studying the late (and more difficult) starter provides an added insight into the more intractable problems to which training designers have recently turned their attention.

1. TEACHING A HIGH-SPEED MANUAL SKILL

One of the commonest jobs for women in industry is that of sewing-machinist. The clothing industry is largely dependent on the women it can recruit and train and the standards of efficiency they can achieve. But the job of sewing-machinist is subject to a severe limitation. Nearly all firms in the industry depend on the recruitment of teenagers. The maximum age at which a job applicant can be economically recruited and trained is normally thought to be 25 to 30. This attitude is common both in the United Kingdom and in other industrial countries of which we have knowledge. It is also significant that several 'progressive' companies have endeavoured to waive the traditional prejudice against acceptance of older trainees and have for a period recruited adults over a wider age span, only to abandon their experiments in the light of further experience. One of the largest 'multiples', as the result of such experience, now has a definite policy never to engage anyone over the mid-20s.

Another large clothing factory, John Barran Ltd, had one of its factories in Gateshead. The company's plans for an expansion of output were being limited by the availability of skilled machinists. The manager of the factory, Mr. M. Stoner, met some of the ITRU research team at an industrial conference in London and was keen to examine the possibilities of solving his labour problem by recruiting adults.

An agreement was reached whereby the research team would endeavour to design and apply a new training programme and the company would recruit a number of older women as trainee sewing-machinists. In fact, it proved remarkably difficult for the company to fulfil its part of the bargain. Constant prodding of the employment exchange, together with advertisements directed at older women, produced very little response. It soon became evident that the notion that middle-aged adults are too old to learn machining in the clothing industry is as firmly rooted amongst working-class women in an area in which the clothing industry is well-established as it is amongst the managers.

After several attempts, only one older person was recruited —Mrs. Chatton, a 50-year-old without industrial experience. Nearly all her adult life had been spent as a housewife and mother of a large family and her only occupational experience before marriage was as a domestic servant and cleaner in a hospital.

Mrs. Chatton was unsuitable on almost every criterion. Her age was regarded as ridiculous for a trainee, and her personality was one of cheerfulness and gentleness. She had a remarkable propensity for philosophy (expressed in the poems she wrote while in the training school!) which was as well, because only her natural qualities of patience, endurance, and cheerfulness sustained her during the many setbacks she encountered.

She did not become the focus of special study and training until she had spent eight weeks in the training school under traditional instruction. At the end of that period she was regarded as hopeless and the instructors confidently expressed their opinions that she would never succeed. So not only was she prejudged as being too old to learn but this seemed confirmed in the event.

The training course at Barran's consisted of preliminary exercises on paper, using an unthreaded machine, followed by practice at four basic seams using a threaded machine and small rectangles of cloth. School-leavers normally completed the course in four or five weeks. After her eight weeks, Mrs. Chatton still had not completed the preliminary exercises. She just could not achieve a reasonable speed of working. On one particular exercise, school-leavers attain the target time of five minutes in about four days; Mrs. Chatton could do no better than seven minutes after ten days. Such failure was repeated with every exercise.

After such a prolonged and fruitless struggle with the training exercises, the first requirement was to renew the trainee's interest. Despite failing the early exercises, she had been allowed to try the later 'seams' exercises. This made it practicable to train her for an actual production job.

Lack of speed in favour of accuracy

Discussion with the instructors about Mrs. Chatton's performance in the preliminary training showed that an inability to work sufficiently quickly was the feature that most characterized her general lack of progress. Her passion was to work meticulously, but, realizing also that she had to build up speed, she tried to combine the two. The result was that she succeeded in neither.

The trainee's limitations came to light further when she started on the specific job on which she was required to train —that of making pockets. At every stage she showed a disposition to pause for extra checks and inspections. Allied to this was her tendency to make alignments which were not strictly necessary. For example, when assembling two pieces ready for sewing, it is usually a waste of time to align them completely before starting to machine: by the time the first few stitches have been put in, the rest will have fallen out of alignment anyway. The correct technique is to align only that part which goes into the machine first. Once that part has been sewn, the rest can then be aligned.

But while it was apparent that the trainee placed a great emphasis on taking pains and showing care and consideration at every move, it was also evident that her performance was poor on anything that necessitated careful discrimination. She tended to confuse components, known as bearers and jettings, which vary in shape but are sometimes quite similar, and she was inclined to get into difficulties with the opposite sides of a pocket by getting one of the pieces the wrong side up.

Some of her problems in cloth handling were equally subtle and of a type that is very liable to escape the attention of those supervising training. Much of the machinist's work is taken up with the handling of cloth and this sometimes entails assembling one piece of cloth (a lining) on top of another. The best technique is to hold the two pieces of cloth independently and then to slide the top one into position over the lower piece. But the trainee tended to lose time in pressing them together first before adjusting the relative positions of the two pieces.

Another instance of a key feature in the skill lies in 'aiming' the foot of the machine before pressing down the treadle. If the foot is aimed in the right direction, the machine can be operated for a long run. But if it is not well aimed, it may be necessary to stop the machine almost immediately. It is all too easy to align the cloth and press down the treadle without giving due regard to the exact positioning of the foot.

Unfortunately, Mrs. Chatton did not naturally adopt the correct method; she had almost a perverse preference for in-efficient procedures. A major problem of communication at once presented itself because, in spite of her patience and efforts to maintain her good humour, it was clear that there was a danger in giving her too much correction. Awareness of mistakes tended to undermine her confidence in her ultimate ability to succeed. Yet how otherwise could she be led along the right path.

Slow-motion teaching

A solution ultimately suggested itself in the adoption of a slow-motion method. By this procedure, the job was broken down in easy stages and for each stage the differences were shown between a good performance and other forms of less efficient performance. This could be demonstrated slowly. But it was even more important that a trainee should perform the first sequences herself very slowly. This served two pur-poses. First, it lightened the load. She could spend plenty of time ensuring that she was doing the right thing without running into any other form of stress. Secondly, it afforded the instructor ample opportunity to check that the right method was being employed. In a high speed task, a slight departure from an ideal method—resulting in, say, a re-grasp of the material—is easily missed and so is likely to be built-in as a bad habit.

The slow-motion method makes the trainee's task less com-plex and gives her more insight into the nature of the skill. Yet it takes some time for someone, who hitherto has been pressed towards greater speed, to accept that a really slow performance is now required. It almost seemed a deli-berate hoax. Mrs. Chatton had to be persuaded repeatedly that her slow performance had to be slowed even further.

It was interesting to record that once the ideal method was performed slowly a few times by Mrs. Chatton, she experienced little difficulty with the element subsequently. Most of the difficulties that were experienced stemmed from a failure to establish the correct pattern in the first place. This evidence is very much in line with that available from psychological studies of older learners, in which the tendency is noted for errors, once committed, to recur with great persistence. The need to avoid errors in the early stages of manual skills seems critical.

Pacing method increases speed

One of the factors preventing improvement on the difficult parts of the task was the trainee's unawareness of just how much time is lost by pausing for extra checks and inspection. To the instructor, with one eye on the stopwatch, it is all too apparent. To make this differentiation equally clear to the trainee, the whole task was broken down into sub-tasks lasting five to fifteen seconds each. The trainee was then told how she had performed on each sub-task as it was finished. From this, it was a short step to reading-off aloud, as the trainee worked, the time left for the current sub-task. The trainee was encouraged to reach the required speed even at the expense of quality.

This method (referred to as 'pacing') brought about far more improvement than had been achieved by verbal instruction. Not only did it improve performance on the difficult parts of the job for which it had been intended, but it further improved those parts where instruction had been successful.

The fact that performance showed such a sudden improvement whenever pacing was introduced indicated that Mrs. Chatton found it stimulating and motivating. But the effects of things stimulating and motivating usually wear off. One might readily have supposed that Mrs. Chatton would fail to keep it up. In fact she kept going. More than that, her times steadily improved, which implied a real gain in skill.

The combination of 'slow motion training' and the 'pacing method' offered a flexible way of helping Mrs. Chatton to improve. The instructor had in his possession two tools, one for getting her to acquire the right technique and the other for getting her up to target speed. He could use them just as he wished according to the progress she was making. There was no point in aiming at the target if the technique had not been mastered. But once the correct method was established (sometimes after a few tries), it was possible to tackle the target time for the sub-task. It was very encouraging for Mrs. Chatton to find that she was reaching a skilled worker's time, if only on small parts of the job.

But the real value of pacing lay more in its application to the combining of elements of work. Parts of the operation which were responsible for lost time were immediately revealed. Instead of finding that an overall cycle time compared unfavourably with the target cycle time, the instructor and learner were shown clearly the part where she had fallen behind. Mrs. Chatton became quicker at recognizing faulty technique after a poor run and readily discussed points with the instructor. If any real problems arose, the difficulty was sorted out by reverting to slow motion. The pacing method seemed to bring the prospects of success only a few seconds away, irrespective of how far Mrs. Chatton had progressed through the total cycle.

After a week of training by the pacing method, Mrs. Chatton had made so much progress that she was considered good enough to leave the school and start work on the production line. But it seemed that Mrs. Chatton's confidence in herself had not yet become firmly established; added to which the production supervisors viewed her transfer from the training school to the production department with some scepticism. On the production line she became tense and she reverted to the extreme care and caution, out of fear of producing spoiled work, that she had shown when first entering the training school.

The deterioration in Mrs. Chatton's performance owed something, too, to the vicissitudes of the factory floor. It so happened that the machine which she was using started to give her trouble. The thread is always liable to break on a sewing machine, but on her machine it started breaking with undue frequency. This contributed significantly to the stress of the change. It broke up her rhythm, and on the work elements subsequent to the thread-breaks her performance fell from the standard achieved earlier.

Joint school and production experience

It was plain that it was not possible for her to keep up with the operations on the conveyer belt without bringing her back again into the training school. She was not officially removed from the production department, but her place on the belt was taken by an experienced worker for two or three hours each day. This relief permitted continued practice at the efficient methods already learned to prevent the consolidation of those less desirable that were developing on the production line. This procedure allowed Mrs. Chatton to reach the stage at which her output and quality were reaching acceptable standards on the line.

At this point another serious blow befell her and, indeed, the whole experiment. The production line changed. Her own particular job disappeared. Others were being developed in their place, but the change necessitated learning a new job. In spite of her philosophic disposition and her desire to fulfil the confidence the instructor had placed in her, she could not face another change.

Younger trainees benefit from the new techniques

By industrial criteria the experiment failed. It seemed that the doom which had been foretold had duly come to pass. Yet it had come tantalizingly near to success. The obvious need was to start the experiment again with several older people. The firm advertised again, help was sought from, and every assistance was given by, the employment exchange. But a boom in jobs in the area at that time did not help and the next set of trainees were, as usual, all young and mostly straight from school. Ironically they became the recipients of training methods especially designed for older adults. Nevertheless, the performances of these trainees showed substantial improvements on any previous young group both in terms of their speed in getting on to production and of the small labour wastage during training.

Perfecting technique before acquiring speed

Mrs. Chatton's difficulties provided the lessons for the continued development of the training scheme. A series of miniaturized whole tasks in which the perfection of technique was followed by the build-up of speed replaced the fragmented exercises and sub-tasks on which speed had been stressed from the outset and on which faulty technique had inevitably been acquired.

The new training programme was then prepared and applied in the clothing factory in Haverhill of D. Gurteen & Sons Ltd. This firm, too, had difficulty in recruiting any older trainees, although once again the programme proved successful with young trainees. Eventually the experiment was transferred to Pasolds Ltd clothing factory in Slough, which recruited women over a wider age range than is usual in the industry. Here the scheme was very successful and it has been adopted by all the company's subsidiary factories in other parts of the United Kingdom.

So Mrs. Chatton made her mark. The older trainee may pose real and formidable problems in some training areas. Meeting the challenge is a means not only of widening the intake to training, but of discovering something deeper about where the problems of training really lie.

2. BREAKING THE ILLITERACY BARRIER

Harry was a maintenance engineer in his mid-30s working

for a large dairy. He had a wife and two children; a boy aged 11 and a girl aged 5. He had a good memory, a skilled job, and liked doing '...anything with my hands'. This last assertion was borne out by the way he kept his house—in perfect decorative order. The one important difference between Harry and his neighbours was that he could not read or write. Only by his exceptional memory did he succeed in keeping his job.

If Harry was illiterate, he did not lack ability. He could converse engagingly and what he had to say seemed thoughtful and sensible. He gained a score of thirty-eight out of a possible sixty on a Raven's Matrices test (involving non-verbal reasoning), which put him a little above average for electrical workers of his particular age group.

Harry attributed his failure to read at school to poor teaching. But the circumstances of his boyhood suggest other explanations. He was 7 when World War II began. His education was continuously interrupted by various events including the death of both parents. For a while he attended an open-air school where the emphasis was on health rather than on academic progress. Harry's interests soon became fixed on craft work.

Effects of illiteracy

It was not until he left school that Harry realized his problems—avoiding the scorn of 'friends' and 'workmates' who thought they were so much better by virtue of being able to read.

Those who cannot read experience difficulties in life that others can scarcely envisage. It is not only a question of cultural deprivation—of being unable to write letters or read newspapers and books. Since place names are unintelligible to the illiterate, there are immense complications in such mundane activities as a visit to an unfamiliar town by train or looking for the right bus—and street maps will be of little use. Illiterates are dependent on asking advice from others, while disguising if possible the reason why they need help. Harry could not fill in forms. He had always 'forgotten his glasses' when persuading someone else to help him. Like most illiterates, Harry not unnaturally became withdrawn and lacking in confidence.

The problems are even more acute with a man who has to find a job. Most jobs demand at least some ability to read or write. Harry was fortunate, for in spite of his handicap, he managed to learn a skilled job which involved servicing complicated machinery. He was able to do this because he possessed a remarkable memory; when shown a new machine he would memorize the instructions and trace a fault on the machine rather than look up the 'symptoms' in a manual.

This is an example of what Harry was supposed to be reading:

'With either auto valves 10 or 10/1 depressed, air is fed from the poppet valve 4, (located so that it is depressed by the traverse carriage when over the bottle conveyor)

(a) through the auto valves to the "bottles in position" trip lever and valve 9, through the 1 cycle valves 8 and 8/1 to operate the grips relay 16 into the "on".

(b) to pilot "bottle stop pilot control valve" to make a clearway from 12 to 14 (no air).'

To avoid the necessity of writing out reports on his work, Harry would find something else which 'had to be done' while someone else wrote the report. Although he had sometimes to contend with scorn from those who discovered that he could not read, he silenced them by pointing out that he could do the job as well—or better—than they could, even though he lacked their skill at reading.

In spite of the fact that he managed fairly well without being able to read, Harry did try to remedy the situation. First he went to evening classes, but says he made no progress, and soon transferred to the craft classes which seemed 'more in my line'. His liking for practical hobbies led to the rather strange situation of his developing a flair for poster

design. Given the wording, he would design and make posters
—without necessarily knowing what the words meant.
Another attempt to read was made when a cousin offered to
teach him—but again without success. Even with individual
attention, the skill seemed to elude him and Harry soon lost
interest.

It was a friend at work who finally persuaded Harry to try
again, by pointing out that to progress in his job and earn
promotion, he simply must be able to read. So he introduced
Harry to Mr. Kilgannon—a headmaster in Oldham who was
running small classes for illiterates and using the then new
Pitman initial teaching alphabet (i.t.a.) and agreed to accom-
pany him to the classes.

Harry's first letter

DER SIR

I am Pleoz to see
that I av red three red Buks
and I av red three yelle Buks
so that will be 36 Buks. in hull
up to now so I will leev you
for now to reed a nother Buk.
so I wil leev you for now.

yars trulee

But before Harry really had a chance to get started, the
friend was transferred to another district. Harry hadn't the
confidence to go to the classes on his own. The fact that they
were twenty miles from his home didn't help.

After a few months Harry had cause to think again. How right his friend had been. You certainly *don't* get promotion at work if you can't read. Harry was passed over for a supervisory appointment in favour of a younger man, whom Harry had helped to train. Harry thought that this man had less experience and skill, but *he* could read, an essential requirement for a foreman's job.

Necessary motivation

This rejection motivated Harry to make a fresh start. At first he was rather hesitant about approaching Mr. Kilgannon again and very conscious of his attendance lapse on the previous occasion. He was soon reassured once he was there, and with his new determination to get promotion the next time a vacancy occurred, he made good progress.

For the next four months, Harry travelled the twenty miles each fortnight for a lesson. He took reading books home and, fortunately, his family did all they could to help (although his son was inclined to be a bit impatient if Harry forgot something he'd already been taught!).

Developing self-confidence

Harry was learning to read and he was getting on with his writing; but this is only one aspect of his 'success story'. Mr. Kilgannon noticed personality changes. He was becoming more confident, a little more forceful and more aware of his own potential. He was very enthusiastic about the i.t.a. system and had no qualms about the change over to the orthodox alphabet, known as traditional orthography (t.o.). He felt now that he was capable not only of learning to read but of getting promotion if it came his way.

Unfortunately, when Harry was just prepared to change to t.o., his attendance at the classes lapsed again. Harry was keen and interested and eager to learn. So why would he stop when success was so near? In fact, it was his wife, not Harry, who was directly responsible for his withdrawal, although in-

After eight lessons

Dear Mr

Kilgonon & Jones.

You will not beleave it.
but the Silenca, on my car
has blowne. so I will not
be able to cam to Schoole
on thursday, has pranised.
and I hove been very bisey at
work with wane thing and an
ether. so I will see you in
the New year if you could I
would be thankfull if you
would send me some Books
as my wife has promised to

P.S.

Help me with them.
wishing you all the very
best for Xmas and New year.

yours Truley

directly it was the fault of ITRU's investigation. We had
interviewed Harry at his home. He was really quite flattered
by the interest we were taking in him and declared his willingness to help others in the same situation. An open invitation
was extended to come again, with a telephone number so that
we could contact him at work. Unfortunately, his wife formed
a less benign interpretation of our visit. She suspected that
the interview and the Raven's Matrices test had been admin-
istered to assess Harry's sanity.

For two months Harry stayed away from his classes. Eventually his desire to progress overcame his wife's misgivings
and he returned to his lessons. This time we kept well away
from the scene. It was only in the last few weeks before this
book was despatched to the publishers, when a few final
points had to be checked with Mr. Kilgannon, that we heard
the latest news. Harry had been promoted to manager.

Poor readers in the population

The story of Harry is somewhat arresting because of the
extent of his educational deprivation. There is unlikely to be
any sizeable group of 'Harrys' who might be debarred from
promotion by total illiteracy. The latest available figures indicate that less than 1 per cent of 15-year-olds leaving school
could be classified as illiterate (failing to reach a reading age
of $6\frac{1}{2}$). But those whose reading abilities are poor rather than
non-existent are quite numerous. In 1956, the semi-illiterates
(with reading ages up to $8\frac{1}{2}$) constituted 4 per cent of all 15-
year-olds and the backward readers (with reading ages up to
$11\frac{1}{2}$) a further 21 per cent.

A minimum reading age of 12 has been suggested as necessary to enable an individual to participate fully in the life of
the community. Hence a substantial minority of the adult
population must be subject to a real handicap. While only
one in 10,000 is truly illiterate, being totally unable to read
or write, possibly as many as one in fifty can read only occasional words, and up to 15 per cent have inadequate reading

or writing skills. An estimated three million adults in Britain
need remedial education in literacy, according to Peter Clyne,
researching for the Russell Committee in Adult Education,
who defines literacy as being able to read and comprehend the
front page of a tabloid newspaper.

Poor reading ability is likely to be combined with an aver-
sion for reading. We may not be conscious of a large body
of backward readers in our midst, but we are all too familiar
with the many who claim to hate paper work. The following
is a quotation from A. Roberts's booklet published by the
Institute of Personnel Management in 1966 entitled *Retraining Older Men in the Art of Writing*:

> ' "Can't abide writing."
>
> 'These words were expressed in exasperation as Tom,
> red in the face, flung down his pen. "I'll do anything but
> write. I'll do the job anytime. I'll talk about it. I'll tell you
> all about it, but I just can't write it! I *never* write!"
>
> ' "You never write?"
>
> ' "No, never!"
>
> ' "What about ordinary needs of life, writing to friends
> and relatives, dealing with business affairs?"
>
> ' "No, my wife does all that. She writes all the letters, does
> all the writing that's needed. That's why I married her!
> That's her job!" '

Fifty-year-old Tom was not alone in his experience. Roberts
goes on to describe another man on the course for Report
Writing—Alfred. Alfred had never owned a pen or pencil...

> ' "Have no use for one, never had to write since I left
> school!" '

It is heartening to read on in Roberts's article that these two
men—and seventeen others like them—eventually '...devel-
oped confidence in written expression...'

Other literacy schemes

Backwardness in reading may well underlie the inability of a stratum of the population to make any form of occupational advancement or even adjustment. (The proportion of backward readers is relatively high, for example, in a prison population.) A small number of people do sterling work in helping to overcome the deficiency. One example is a literacy scheme in South-East London. A panel of part-time tutors operates in thirty-one districts around London. Many of the cases that come to them are precipitated by the hardship that illiteracy causes. One woman with two children but no husband would not draw National Assistance because she was scared of the office finding out that she could not read forms and sign her name. A man walked two miles to work every day because he could not read the names on the buses.

Evening remedial reading and writing classes for adults were begun by the Surrey County Council in the Chertsey area in 1968. In two years, the scheme developed to include six classes with over 45 students of both sexes ranging in age from 15 to 55. With four teachers, the small groups created an atmosphere of personal attention. The classes fall into three distinct groups; beginners, intermediate and advanced. The teacher-in-charge attributes much of the success of the scheme to the initial assessment of a student's ability, which ensures that work is started at just the right level.

Much of the work is based on individual taped programmes and a comprehensive system is being developed which includes reading, writing, spelling, comprehension, and verbalization. The i.t.a. is not used, as the teacher believes that transfer problems might add to the student's difficulties.

The i.t.a. and older learners

Let us return to Mr. Kilgannon. How is it that he was successful in teaching Harry when others had failed? Was there something about Mr. Kilgannon? His first pupil with the initial teaching alphabet was a girl of 20. She too was a good worker who was offered promotion in her firm. The welfare officer realized her difficulties and tried to teach her to read, but without success. She then went along to Mr. Kilgannon. Within five weeks she was reading i.t.a. and within another five was reading a woman's magazine.

Mr. Kilgannon has tried t.o. with adults but with less success. Perhaps the i.t.a. starts with an advantage in that it offers contrast from something that had apparently failed earlier. It offers, too, some quick results in the early stages and this may restore confidence. Yet such general research information as we have available suggests that the i.t.a. is no more effective than t.o. in the remedial teaching of adults even though it has advantages with young children.

To quote Mr. Kilgannon, '... motivation must be provided for the illiterate before success can be achieved—even with i.t.a. The fundamental significance of this learning medium is its logic and consistency. Allied to individual motivation, success is almost inevitable...'

Reading between the lines of Harry's case history, and recognizing the crucial moments in his progress, another factor can be detected—the understanding support of a friend or tutor prepared to encourage or help without condescension.

3. KEEPING SUPERVISORS UP-TO-DATE

All too often in industry it is said of a supervisor that 'he has become difficult and unco-operative of late' or 'he is not really up to the job now—he was promoted too rapidly and cannot keep pace with new techniques and ideas'. The practical difficulties of helping these allegedly difficult and 'conservative' foremen must seem almost insurmountable.

This case study was made at Clarks Ltd, a shoemaking company established 150 years ago. In the last thirty years it has expanded enormously; in 1939 it employed comparatively few highly skilled craftsmen in one town, Street, in Somerset, but by 1969 it was a substantial company employing 7,000 people in fifteen factories in the South-West of England. The considerable increase in size, and the acceleration in the use of complex machinery, is continuing. Until ten years ago the supervisors were mainly recruited from the shop floor, and, therefore, were men skilled in the traditional techniques of shoemaking. Each supervisor had a wide range of responsibility; constraints such as production planning were informal. A foreman could usually meet a sudden demand for increased output or shorter delivery dates by calling for extra effort from his operators or using up some of his 'buffer' stock. In the past ten years, however, there have been so many changes in the company that the role of the supervisor has been revolutionized.

The increasingly competitive market for footwear has made it essential for all firms to make the most effective use of the assets invested in production and to reduce working capital to the minimum. Pressure to reduce or remove buffer stocks within the factory and between operators has exposed the supervisor to the consequences of mismanagement and unforeseen events. A new urgency has developed to plan more precisely the output of the section and to foresee all possible contingencies.

Equally important has been the need to make the most effective use of labour. Although work study was introduced to Clarks in the early 1950s, the 1960s onwards saw an increasing precision of application in methods, standards and timings of jobs. The supervisor had to be more exact in determining reasons for lost time, and this may have persuaded management to use work-study men rather than supervisors as their target-setters.

Technology also changed the supervisor's task. Synthetic materials and plastics were used in increasing quantities. Machines were becoming more complex, and required more careful specification of materials and much more careful setting up before satisfactory results could be obtained.

The end result of many of these changes was a reduction in process times, fewer operations and fewer machines, thus giving more space, introduction of conveyors in all sections, and the greater specialization of units. The supervisor's responsibility became narrower, but his performance could be measured much more precisely. He needed the ability to integrate his work with his fellow supervisors and play a part as a member of the management team.

Management retraining

The training of men to fill new vacancies presented no particular problem to Clarks who had a supervisory training programme and were aware of the need to prepare for succession.

However, the established supervisors saw the changes and the emergence of the new supervisors as a threat to their position and status. They believed, often correctly, that their departments had dwindled and that there were many people 'treading on their toes'. They found it difficult to work effectively with the increasingly large and ever more expert service departments. It was this group of established supervisors who were now being drawn into the company's retraining programme.

Some of the retrainees were described as follows:

'Very experienced, but unenthusiastic, set in his ways, not progressive enough. Although he was promoted quickly from the shop floor to supervisory staff, for several years now has "stood still"—because of this he gives the impression of not caring.'

'Ex Grammar school, determined, delightful personality but a "yes-man"—not making a very effective contribution.'

'Tremendous experience of the company, wise and knowledgeable in technology but superficially appears lazy and "couldn't care less"—a source of irritation to those who do not see his real worth.'

'Was a very good chargehand and therefore appointed to foreman but has failed in creating the management thinking and sort of general aura required of him.'

'Started as operator from school at the age of 14. Quickly promoted to chargehand, then to under-foreman during war-time expansion. Lack of technical knowledge became apparent—attended classes. Not able to implement changes, resentful of colleagues' suggestions.'

'With the company since leaving the Forces. Has helped to start up three new lines in two factories but has had no formal training.'

Method study course

It was out of the question for the company to 'write off' these men as 'useless' on the grounds that their job knowledge and experience were no longer relevant to current materials, methods and organization. The real need was to impart a better understanding of current production methods and to afford a proper appreciation of their own role and a sense of the special contribution they could make to the future of the company. But how? The final decision was to develop a retraining course around the method study section of the curriculum used for trainee work study engineers. This would afford opportunity for discussion of the new techniques and their effect upon organization, and would lead the men, through the practical work included in the course, towards an integration of this knowledge with their own experience.

The head of work study was made responsible for drawing up the details of the syllabus and for the conduct of the course. Retraining groups were kept as small as possible, the first three courses each comprising no more than four trainees. There is no record of anyone declining the offer and, whilst none of the first four seemed very clear about the object of their attendance, they all believed that it had something to do with personal development which would be to their advantage.

The first part of the course comprised method study. The necessary mathematics for this included the use of a slide rule; an appreciation of time study; and a short project to be carried out by two 'trainees' working together on one project and occasionally guided by a qualified member of the work study department. Ample opportunity occurred during this part of the course to discuss the changes which had taken place in the company, the problems arising out of the use of new materials, and the methods of resolving these problems. No rigid time-table was laid down for the eight weeks devoted to this part of the course, because it was thought that the situation allowed sufficient flexibility to proceed at the pace of the 'trainees'. It would have been upsetting to the group to find that they were slipping behind schedule and this would have frustrated the 'therapy' of the course.

During the second part of the course, each 'trainee' set out on his own to undertake a longer project in one of the company's other factories. These projects were much-needed investigations into problems such as the causes of 'bottle-necks'. They required five- to six-months' study, and the 'trainee' was required to report his findings and recommendations to higher management. During his project he had access to the course tutor for advice in times of difficulty, and occasionally he was visited on the job by the tutor who watched progress. Magnetic boards and blocks representing machines and equipment were used to examine probable changes in plant layout. Programmed instruction figured in lessons on basic mathematics and the use of a slide rule.

After attending these courses, six of the men resumed their supervisory appointments, two holding more responsible jobs than formerly. Four returned to a similar supervisory status but they have been re-enthused and are in line again for further promotion.

Two 'retrainees' have shown ability for work study practice. They have subsequently completed the full work study training course and are now competent work study engineers within the company.

Another 'retrainee' is in charge of product development in one of the factories. The pace of direct production appeared to be crushing him but once these pressures were lifted 'a thinking man emerged'.

Another is in charge of process control and development. His assistant is the 'retrainee' who started retraining without knowing what a decimal point was, and is now said to be doing a first rate job.

At this point, ITRU interviewed some of the supervisors concerned. What emerged was new light on the effect of this 'late' training on their general outlook on life and on the importance they attached to retraining in helping to reorientate themselves. This had not come about suddenly, but had developed slowly, founded on a general sense of dissatisfaction with themselves or with their lot.

Logical approach

Tony Howard, aged 42, exemplifies this experience:

> 'I felt I was getting in a rut in shoemaking so I decided to take a course with the Somerset County Council. My factory superintendent must have heard and made arrangements for me to go on to the company course. This put my shoemaking background to use in a way that was realistic. One tended to jump to decisions before, but afterwards I realized that unless you look at things logically, basically with a work study trained mind, you are apt to get the wrong answers. I found this training allowed me to harness the little shoemaking knowledge I had to give better results. Now I would seize any opportunity I felt I could benefit from, a course, a move, even a lecture; I think knowledge is fine.'

Not all the supervisors had the same initial urge to be retrained. Tom Burroughs, also 42, was frank about the way he started, as he went on the course through there being no other job available at the time. He was also worried about his minimal education and lack of travel outside Street except for war service in the RAF, for which he volunteered, entering as a shoemaker and ending as a fitter. However, he enjoyed the course once he had overcome his first apprehension.

'I think you really need to get settled in; then you get to the stage about three or four days later when you want to go on and see what it's all about. But I think it was confined too much to the shoemaking industry; it should have also covered what people do in other industries. In this place you tend to think in shoes and shoes only, but I am sure that there is a lot to be learned by looking at other industries and then applying it to the shoemaking industry. I would have thought that a break of this sort, say once a week, just for half a day to visit another industry, would have been useful.

'Another thing I felt was lacking was the way to deal with people from outside that you had to meet. I am thinking of people like representatives who come in and try to sell various components. You have to deal with them, and you have to be careful. This was something that could have been covered, but was not included in the course at all.

'But the course as a whole did me good—there is no doubt about it. It straightened my way of thinking, it alerted me to possibilities. It made me less apprehensive; this was taught on the course to a certain extent, in as much as you often had to stand up and speak on all sorts of subjects when your turn came. This sort of thing is good, especially with people who haven't had any experience of talking in public, because I think my job consists of talking to people.'

Speed of learning

Ralph Munsey is 56. He had been running a welting line for nearly ten years and was one of those chosen for the first course. He was one of the supervisors who stressed the specific content of the course in terms of the benefits which a knowledge of work study offered. But it was not only that.

'I thought it would be a good opportunity to learn. We found it hard for the first week, especially the slide rule and calculations. Your brain hadn't been used to this sort of thing. After the first week we found it came quite easily, with a little bit of practice. Another problem was slowing down; after being on a production line you wanted to do everything too quickly. Perhaps you did not stop and think. You make snap decisions in a factory. After you have stopped to think you find that there are two or three methods of doing a job, and then by incorporating the two or three different methods you come out with a better one. If, for example, you were going to put in a new job— before you put it in, perhaps you would think about it for a couple of days, get a method out, lay it out on paper, and perhaps pick out the best of the different methods you had, and then use that. This, I find, trained me to stop and think.

'I would recommend this course for anyone, but I would say that you must have the right type of instructor. When you are middle-aged, I think you must have someone who is going to talk your own language. Also, I do not think you can be hurried so much when you are middle-aged as you can when you're young. You don't seem to grasp things quite as quickly as a younger chap. But this course was put over in a friendly way, like having a talk in a pub.'

Ralph Munsey also gained confidence from having to talk on set subjects, and now has no troubles over addressing groups. Moreover, he now applies the work study techniques to other projects, including domestic redecorating. However, he had one further important point.

'When you have had this course and go back into the factory, you are thinking differently. This is damned hard unless everybody has had this kind of instruction and training.... People get your back up, because you know what you're doing and they aren't working by the same method. They want everything quick, the traditional approach. So it's no good just a few having this course.'

Dave Blount is an instructor who was responsible for the interviewees and others who passed through the retraining programme for supervisors. He did not *feel* the experience which retraining offered the men, but he observed it with objectivity and with the perceptiveness of one who is struck by the special needs of the middle-aged trainee.

'I believe that very few companies have gone in for this sort of thing. When we started off we had problem foremen, about four or five around the company who had got flat and stale, and we decided to bring them on to an extended training course. We chose work study as the vehicle, but it might as well have been allotment planning. When I became involved, we were groping in the dark. Nobody quite knew what we were up to and these chaps were a little bit like goldfish in a bowl: everyone came to look at them. The position was made more difficult because they kept worrying, "what's going to happen to us afterwards?" Frankly we didn't know ... in fact we expanded throughout the 1950s at such a colossal rate that we were glad for anyone to wear a white coat. It was very rewarding because they were so pathetically eager. They were so eager and keen to do well that we gave them something difficult— work study. In fact it was so difficult for some of them that I had to sit down and teach one chap decimals before we could make any progress at all. I had several of them coming

round to my house in the evenings for tutorials. They were
that keen. In the end it turned out well. Initially, we concentrated on maths training because some of the men were
not as good as they might have been. By and large these
people were re-enthused and went on to bigger things.

'The man who was once my senior foreman was capable
of a much bigger job than he was doing. The work study
manager and I sat here one day and said to him: "This is
your last chance". That chap has now a very responsible
job in one of our factories. He went into work study as a
job. From there he was put in charge of process control for
the factory... Like most problems in life it is not the solution that is difficult. It is identifying the situation and the
problem. A work study course is a good vehicle to use, but
what matters is getting someone on a course where you can
give him individual treatment... You give him a chance
to talk and you give him redirection if it's due.'

One remarkable feature about this group of supervisors was
the general effect of the course on their outlook and personality. The torpid, routine-bound, and uninvolved had become lively, resourceful, constructively minded, ready for
anything, including further courses if the opportunity offered.

This reawakening seemed to spring from three particular
aspects of the training which excited them:

1. The necessity from time to time of 'saying their piece':
   an illustration of the transforming power of encouraging
   men to express their thoughts, feelings and intentions—
   and their problems.

   They were all countrymen, previously not much given to
   speech, used to expressing themselves through their skills
   and routines. The interview material recorded on tape
   showed them quite unusually articulate, with very flexible
   command of vocabulary, and syntax, and a lively mode of
   expression.

2. The introduction to work study: the tool of management

most conspicuous on the shop floor, but arcane and suspect
to the operative and charge-hand. These men had been
inducted into a 'mystery' and the new knowledge spelt
almost magical power.

3. The use of the slide rule for mathematical exercises became the source of delight and pride; another mystery of
which they had been made masters.

Out of competence in these three fields their confidence
had grown and zest was awakened. Perhaps it was no longer
true to say 'there's nothing like leather'. These men thought
there was nothing like work study for enlivening them and
widening their perspectives.

GUIDE TO ACTION

Trainees who are regarded as over-age in their training
environments sometimes progress so well that age is seen as
no more than an arbitrary convention of little relevance to an
individual's suitability for training. But often an isolated
experience with an older starter is associated with a set-back
and serves to reinforce the argument, perhaps temporarily
forgotten, for rigorous age discrimination. It would be easier
to maintain a more flexible policy on the matter of the age
of entry into training, if training officers were more aware of
and ready to meet the expected difficulties of the late starter.

Developing a work tempo

On manual jobs, older learners tend to engage in over-
meticulous actions which inhibit the development of a satisfactory rate of working, especially if they have no previous
experience of speed-stressed skills. The symptoms often take
the form of an obsession with accuracy. Here several
approaches recommend themselves according to the type of
skill to be acquired:

1. Using a learning method which generates speed at the outset, providing it is not a task which also makes equally stringent demands on accuracy.
2. Forcing the speed on an easy or already acquired part of the task. Speed of performance can be transferred from one set of elements to others.
3. Forcing the pace during learning. This is sometimes necessary where the job done slowly does not provide the same 'feed back' to the senses as it does when performed quickly. For example, certain small imperfections in woven products can often only be detected by rapid scanning movements of the hands.
4. Separating the learning of accuracy and speed wherever precise movements are essential to both. These precise movements can be learned by a slow motion technique until the instructor is satisfied that they are exactly right. Then the speed of the movements is increased.

Overcoming inflexibility

Methods of and attitudes towards work are often transferred from the long established older skill to the new job even when they are unwanted and inappropriate. Training may be no less important in helping an older person to gain some new orientation as in helping him to master some new job procedure, for it is as difficult to unlearn attitudes as it is to learn new work habits. If real changes are to be brought about, the distinguishing features of new job skills and demands need to be emphasized and interest in them cultivated.

Fixing attainable targets

Failure to meet a goal often results in disproportionate depression amongst older trainees, but the crisis can easily be averted by setting targets that are within the bounds of accomplishment after only a limited amount of training and practice. Positive advantages flow from enabling a new trainee to experience an early sense of achievement even if this means distorting schedules and varying the training times allotted to particular tasks. Even so, no stage in training should become unduly protracted. To guard against the plateau effect, to which the older starter is so susceptible, thought should be given to the various ways in which the training momentum can be maintained.

Allowing for individual differences

Variations in individual capacity make the problems of selection and placement of foremost importance over a very wide field of occupations. Questions of aptitude and trainability become of even greater significance as age increases, because individual differences tend to widen. Disuse of functions is lowering the capabilities of some while the cumulative effect of skills developed and maintained is extending capabilities in others. Late starting entails a risk. But the risks are lowered when selection techniques suitable for older starters are employed. The training officer must always be ready to advise on the suitability of candidates for the jobs for which training is provided.

While more discriminating selection will make it easier to apply a standard training programme and offer more certainty in the results, the acceptance of older beginners is likely to increase variability. Difficulties may be specific to particular individuals so that in effect the training officer will spend a large proportion of his time diagnosing individual problems and sorting out the factors that contribute to confusion in application or orientation.

Motivating the under-educated

Some who are brought into training on social, contractual, and other grounds have the double disadvantage of being both older and more poorly educated than the normal intake of trainees and they are consequently likely to be more resistant to training. The first priorities are to engage their interests and to enable them to discover that further education and training can be infinitely more exciting than anything they had expected. The adoption of new methods, techniques, and approaches and the removal of all sources of tension, embarrassment, and self-consciousness will pave the way, and the 'surprise' created may result in the trainees feeling a new lease of life.

4. Slow Beginners

INTRODUCTION: TRAINING PERFORMANCE—JOB PERFORMANCE

At some time, every training programme may encounter a trainee who falls behind the others and fails to progress at a reasonable rate. How should he be regarded? Can it be said: 'He'll never make it?' Or is it worth trying again?

It is commonly believed that a trainee who has difficulty in learning a skill will not be suited to the job itself. If this were so, it would be logical to terminate the training for someone who is struggling on a course. But is it so? There is a good deal of information now to suggest that performance during training is not necessarily a good guide to ultimate performance in production (as judged by a machine efficiency figure, an output bonus, or a supervisor's rating). All this has been brought to the fore in the course of work attempting to validate selection tests. People whose production performance confirms their selection for the job are often those who would be rejected on training grounds, while those who seem potentially suitable for training are sometimes poor long-term prospects as production employees.

This is readily understandable. Performance in training often demands a high verbal comprehension, a retentive and flexible mind and a capacity for sustained concentration. Performance in production, on the other hand, commonly calls for applied effort, reliability and conscientiousness in ensuring quality of work, ingenuity in coping with difficulties, and such social assets as a capacity for team work.

These latter qualities characterize many older and middle-aged workers, who at the same time would be regarded, not without justification perhaps, as inferior material for training. But if the older worker is slower to learn, does it mean that he has less ultimate potential for the job?

Bill Stokes, aged 40, is learning to become a process operator in a South of England refinery. John Campbell, aged 56, is also learning to be a process operator but in a chemical plant in the North East, while Alfred Marne, aged 42, is learning to become a machine operator in the Midlands. All three have something in common—initially they progressed poorly. But they have something else in common: they have now caught up and are on the way to becoming highly regarded in job proficiency.

It would have required only a slight change in circumstances for all three slow learners to have been withdrawn from training and transferred to less responsible work. The material of the training course seemed beyond them. Their difficulties in fact were similar. What they were being taught did not somehow slot into place. The training material seemed to them abstract. At any rate, much of the training passed over their heads.

The fact that all three trainees eventually surpassed expectations cannot be credited as a success story for training. In two of the three cases a fortuitous event provided what was needed; the right stimulus, a realization that what they were learning about made sense, and a recovery of confidence in their own abilities.

But our third case is a different story. Luck came the way of Bill Stokes through 'failure' resulting in his transfer to Peter Davey, a graduate training supervisor, who was given a last chance to do something with him. Peter, an expert in plant operation and knowledge, was less concerned with the orderly presentation of his subject than in finding out what made Bill tick as a learner.

The slow learner is often regarded as a hindrance in a training programme. Perhaps, however, he should be welcomed. For it is by understanding the nature of his difficulties that the training officer learns to appreciate what training is all about.

1. INDUSTRIAL TUTORIALS BREAK SEMANTIC BARRIER

Forty-one-year-old Bill Stokes had an agricultural background and elementary schooling. He became a trainee continuous process operator at a petroleum refinery and had great difficulty in acquiring the uncommon job knowledge and skill required for his new duties. His training (mainly on-the-job training) was in no way assisted by a complex operating manual which he was told to study. This manual and the training reduced him to despair.

The allotted period for training was nine weeks. At the end, a passing out assessment interview was conducted by his plant manager. He failed, and his plant manager decided as a last resort to send him to the department's training centre for two weeks to see if anything could be done for him there.

At the training centre, the training supervisor and the training instructor were able to win the man first to a state of confidence and then to a state of enthusiastic learning.

How this was achieved is described in the following recorded conversation between 'TS' (Peter Davey, the continuous process operator training supervisor at Fawley Refinery) and 'JB' (John Barber, senior lecturer in management studies, Portsmouth Polytechnic, who was formerly a part-time member of ITRU).

JB: I would very much like to hear your assessment of the reasons underlying Bill Stokes' original failure in training. Perhaps we could discuss what he had to learn.

TS: Yes, so we can start then by talking about the job. This involves an ethylene storage sphere with compressors and control mechanism. The sphere receives liquid ethylene and stores it at $-100°C$. From the storage sphere, it is pumped as required to the customers via pipelines. In fact, the operator does not have a lot to do. His actual operations are relatively simple, but the understanding of his job is more difficult to establish. The situation is potentially dangerous. If anything causes the ethylene to start warming up, very high pressures develop.

JB: What exactly is ethylene?

TS: It is an inflammable petroleum gas which liquefies under about 70 kilonewtons per square metre pressure at −100°C. It is kept liquid by its very low temperature.

Although the equipment is therefore covered with various safety devices and control instruments, the real need is to make a man feel confident that he knows what he is handling; that he knows the danger signs. It isn't difficult to teach him his routine operations, but it is difficult to ensure that he knows what he is doing. The skill of the process operator lies in his capacity for diagnosis and that is what distinguishes him from the typical manual worker.

JB: His routine procedures presumably are the turning on and off of valves and other controls in a certain order?

TS: They also include control of lubricating pumps, and interpreting flow measurements—for example, a certain quantity of ethylene from one of the ethylene producing plants passes into his sphere and he has to know the significance of this in terms of whether to start another compressor. So he needs to know both when and how to do this.

One of his duties is to send ethylene from this sphere through a piece of equipment called an evaporator. This heats and vaporizes the ethylene. He needs to know how to commission the evaporator and how to commission the pump. The pump will be at normal atmospheric temperature and he has to chill it gradually to −100°C. He must know how to commission pressure controllers and flow controllers.

These are all routine operations which can be learnt quite easily. The cardinal point about this job is that it isn't enough simply to teach written operations. You also need to instil a fair degree of understanding of the process in order to develop a degree of confidence that permits a man to make his own diagnosis and act on it. It's a key operation. The ethylene sphere is linked with two plants producing ethylene and with pipelines to the customers. Although the process is largely automatic, the operator must know what to do in unusual circumstances—when to be concerned and when not to be concerned.

JB: Tell us something about Stokes.

TS: Well when Stokes came to us he was 41. He had left school at 14 and was very much a local country chap, interested in agricultural matters, horses and things like that. He came from a manual job on the refinery where he had been pushing barrels about. Then, because he hurt his back, he had to be moved to another job. He was sent to this continuous process plant, to learn this job in the traditional way. He was given a manual and was told to pick things up from the other operators, making use of the manual to understand difficult points. After nine weeks he was tested by his supervisor, who in effect said 'this man just doesn't understand anything about the process; he doesn't understand the instrumentation; he doesn't understand what he is dealing with. I can't let him operate this plant.'

JB: The manual then had done very little to help him?

TS: The manual is a detailed description of the plant, written by a graduate engineer for the benefit of the operators, but it takes no account of the difficulties that a man like this trainee might have in trying to sort matters out.

There are many sentences here that I had to read a number of times before I could understand them.

It starts off 'The system will probably receive up to

182 tonnes a day of liquid ethylene at $-20°C$ and at approximately 2550 kN/m^2 from Steam Cracker I, and $-23°C$ and at 2275 kN/m^2 from Steam Cracker II. Liquid ethylene feed is chilled by heat exchange with vapour from the sphere to approximately $-26°C$ and is then flashed to sphere operating pressure. Flashed vapour at $-95°C$ is removed from the sphere by reciprocating compressors. These machines can return up to 75 tonnes a day of ethylene vapour at approximately 2070 kN/m^2 into the chemical product pipeline.'

This is on the front page, by way of preliminary explanation. It goes straight on to 'It is not desirable to operate at liquid run-down rates lower than 50 tonnes a day in winter and probably about 100 tonnes a day in summer. At flow rates below these levels, heat leakage into the line is significant and vapour locks cause erratic flow. This interferes with splitter control on the feeding unit, although due to the nature of its control system Steam Cracker II is far less susceptible than Steam Cracker I to this type of upset. When starting liquid flow into the line, erratic flow must be tolerated until the line is cooled to the operating temperature of approximately $-23°C$'—and so on.

JB: This must have created a terrific semantic barrier for a man already apprehensive about whether he is going to learn a new job. Didn't he turn to the other operators for help?

TS: Yes, but he admitted it was a case of 'the blind leading the blind'.

JB: Meaning that other operators didn't understand it very well either, so that attempts to explain to him what it meant only made matters worse?

TS: He couldn't make sense out of either the manual or the explanations of others. The point is that an operator learning the job sees it only from his own point of view and none of the operators had gleaned much from the manual. It had not been written from their viewpoint, but from the viewpoint of a plant designer trying to get to grips with the things that those who are commissioning a piece of equipment ought to know.

JB: In what sort of mood was Stokes when he was finally passed over to you?

TS: He was very depressed and when I first met him I thought we wouldn't be able to do anything for him at all. We couldn't, until two of us sat down with Stokes and started to talk about and discuss the job in very simple terms.

Candidly, neither myself nor my instructor knew much about the job. What we did was to divide it into little digestible items, and I think the first item we took was the actual storage sphere itself. Another item was the compressors; another was the pumps which take the ethylene away from the sphere; then we took the evaporators. We drew each one of them on charting paper. We first drew the sphere. This is simply a circle within a circle with half-a-dozen or so take-off points on it going to pipelines which ultimately feed other units. We sat down in front of this drawing and I had the operating manual. We looked at the drawing and we asked each other questions about it. We said, for instance: 'Why is it made up of two spheres—an inner sphere and an outer sphere?' and we thrashed round the question.

JB: Is it because the shell acts like a vacuum flask?

TS: Exactly. Then we took another point. The space between the two spheres is purged continuously with nitrogen gas and so we looked at that. It is there to keep the space between the two spheres free from moisture.

'Well now, why is this?' we asked. We all looked at the diagram and said: 'What do we have here? We have these control-valves leading the nitrogen in. We have it going in at these places and then we have a little place where it leads out and a meter where you can measure whether it is flowing. Now why have we got this meter; what is it for; what is it doing?'

There was discussion round that for a while, but the point is Bill Stokes didn't really have much to say. The conversation was mainly between myself and my instructor.

Again we looked at the facts of the job as displayed on the board; the fact that there was nitrogen going in, the fact that there was this inner sphere and an outer sphere. We discussed why ... why is it like this? We asked: 'Why have we got these three safety valves on the nitrogen?' And then we asked: 'What temperature is the stuff in this sphere?', and we went on little by little building up the facts. Then we would go right back to the beginning again and ask the trainee for his comments.

JB: Did he not, by this time, begin to talk? He ought to have been in advance of you in his knowledge, because he had spent nine weeks on the plant.

TS: He contributed very little, but then the point came when suddenly he asked a question and said: 'Well, what is ethylene? Why is it −100°C?'

JB: This is fascinating, because if a man can work nine weeks on an ethylene storage plant and doesn't know what ethylene is, then communication must have broken down somewhere completely. The big thing was that you got him to ask a question.

TS: Yes and we followed it up with a demonstration. We were able to take a light hydrocarbon and show that by reducing the pressure it vaporized while by reducing the temperature the rate of vaporization slowed down. In fact, we were able to demonstrate these relationships to him with water. We took ordinary water in a vessel in which we could pull a partial vacuum. The reduction in pressure caused the water to evaporate very rapidly, so rapidly that it boiled at far below its normal boiling temperature.

Having seen this concept demonstrated he came very

easily to accept it as a fact. 'All right,' he said, 'I have seen it—this is what has happened. I can see now what you are getting at'.

JB: This must have produced a big change in his state of mind. Did it seem to make any difference to his participation or attitude towards learning?

TS: Yes, his whole attitude was transformed. We were working on the theory of digestible amounts, all of which were meaningful. Previously he had been subjected to large amounts—to the whole plant—but he hadn't known where to start or what was what.

JB: You say you were working on small amounts when you were discussing what ethylene is. You were in fact dealing with the basis of the whole by saying, 'Forget all about the plant and think of the process itself'. If we get hold of the concept then all that the plant does fits into place. Once this was clear you could begin to fit in the purpose of all the big pieces of equipment into something like a logical pattern. What happened next?

TS: We got him to understand the vapour pressure course which ethylene takes; to understand the changes in the vapour pressure of liquid ethylene at any temperature. We showed him how to read this from charts and when we came to different pieces of the equipment we would say: 'This sphere is operating at 70 kN/m². What temperature is it going to be at?' We would have him look at his chart and he would say: 'It is going to be —100°C.' We would say: 'All right, when you go up to the plant this afternoon take a look and see if you were right: remember the figure you got from our chart'.

Similarly when we came to another part of the plant diagram where the ethylene was at 2275 kN/m² we would say: 'You look on your chart and tell us what the temperature will be', and he looked and found that the temperature was 16°C. Again we said: 'When you go up to that piece of equipment on the plant, take a look and see for yourself'. (In both cases, the practical check which showed his theoretical work to be correct gave him added confidence.) We made the same approach with the evaporator, where it operates at a particular pressure. Eventually he became quite tickled with this because he felt that there was something in this little graph. He felt he had more than a clue of what to expect; that in fact ethylene was conforming and behaving as the chart and graph led him to expect it to behave.

Every now and again we had to clarify technical terms like flashing. We simply demonstrated what was meant, showing in this case that where liquid at a certain pressure and temperature is shot into a vessel at a lower pressure it turns immediately from liquid to vapour.

This was the next turning point in progress as we found ourselves working on a second principle. We were trying to present to Stokes the facts of the job, the facts of the equipment, the facts of the process, without a tremendous amount of talk. We were aiming at the point in which he would make correct deductions for himself.

JB: In a sense you were removing word barriers created by the lecture method.

TS: Yes, and you can see the contrast when he had learned something from his own experience. After his first trip back to the plant he came back already cheered up. He said: 'Well, I have been staring at that sphere for nine weeks but I never realized what that pressure controller was for', or, 'I never realized that it was important that the pressure between those spheres had to be maintained just so, and that is why we've got a pressure controlling device and an alarm in the control room. I never realized that. I don't think the other operators realized it either, but now I do'.

After slightly less than two weeks of learning by this

method, Stokes returned to the plant and from then on became a very competent operator.

2. SLOW LEARNER—FAST LEARNER

Alfred Marne and George Jenkins were two individuals whose temperaments and learning dispositions were very different. George Jenkins was full of confidence, alert, lively, and dynamic. By contrast, Alfred Marne stood at almost the opposite end of the personality spectrum. He was conscientious but quiet, shy, nervous, and lacking in confidence. Jenkins was 43 and Marne 42 when they were both taken on for training as operators for a bank of automatic roller grinding machines in British Timken, Division of the Timken Roller Bearing Company.

Jenkins was the fast learner. He had no difficulty in picking up his new occupation and achieved a high standard of performance at the end of an eight weeks' course. Marne, the slow learner, had been obliged to undertake the training as he had become redundant in his former job through a change in the pattern of production. He failed to make satisfactory progress in the training course and was transferred to lower grade work in the machine shop where the grinding machines were situated. In due course he got his chance to work under supervision on the grinding machine and eventually became an entirely self-reliant operator and one of the best men in the shop.

These diverse patterns of development prompt questions both about the individuals and the training. Was it a deficiency in Marne or in the training that accounted for the earlier failure? Or was it that Marne was the typical middle-aged trainee and Jenkins the exception? Or had Jenkins, who had trained after Marne, benefited by an improvement in the training?

Before examining what happened to Marne and Jenkins, it is useful to consider the job. The operator responsible for five automatic grinding machines has a certain amount of routine manual work to perform. He must keep the hopper of each grinding machine stocked with rollers for grinding. More demanding is the need for accuracy of measurement in taking spot checks on the rollers with special gauges; but the most skilled work lies in making necessary machine adjustments to maintain specified tolerances. Here, errors, misconceptions or oversights can have costly consequences: but at the same time accurate work should not be achieved at the expense of reasonable machine efficiency. Work of this type clearly calls for the 'man for the job'.

George Jenkins had been a machine operator before he joined the company. He had no experience as a grinder but was well placed to benefit from a course designed to teach him the operation of precision grinding machines. The firm had selected him both for that reason and because he was a man who displayed confidence and initiative.

His supervisor confirmed that from the outset Jenkins had in fact, been 'all right'. His performance had been above average. He had been quick to learn and was keen and hard working.

Jenkins himself paid warm tributes both to his supervisor and to the training method. He explained that training had begun with a day in the workshop near the machines he was ultimately to operate. He spent the second day alongside an experienced grinding machine operator and it was not until the next day that he went to the training classroom. There he was given individual tuition by his course instructor and the opportunity to discuss and to ask as many questions as he liked. On the fourth day he was taken round the factory so that he might see the total production process of which his bank of five machines would be a part. Before starting any further work on the machines he spent a number of days studying drawings and diagrams. Then, after further instruction and job training, he had to take a test to check how far he had followed and understood the instruction up to that stage. Jenkins passed the test without difficulty. He then began a lengthy period of interspersed classroom and on-the-job training which was supervised by a skilled instructor. In total, the training period lasted eight weeks.

The promise shown by Jenkins at his recruitment interview was fulfilled. His work record had been one of success from the first day. It should not, however, be overlooked that he had received a very well planned training course at the hands of a skilled instructor. His final comment about his training was: 'No, I was never afraid of the thought of retraining. It was a very good course and I enjoyed it right from the outset. I never felt nervous about it. I enjoyed it—just as I enjoy my work'.

Throughout the interview, he had spoken in a clear, firm, confident manner. He was not boasting—he was simply being himself.

Lack of confidence slows progress

The case of Alfred Marne is very different. His training had taken place two years earlier before a fully integrated course had been properly planned and developed. His lack of progress after two weeks was such that he had been suspended from training. Later, he had been allowed to start the course a second time. After the passage of two weeks, he was regarded as being much too slow and the shop supervisor intervened out of a sense of realism to press that he should be taken off the course. Only Marne's previous service record with the company saved him. At any rate it led to a compromise solution. Marne would be kept in training, but the end in view was a simple two-man machine in the same department. There Marne remained as second man for a period of six months. After that he 'stood in' as first man. In due course he moved round to other machines and gradually acquired all-round proficiency on machine work in the department.

A request was made to interview Marne but his line supervisor expressed doubt as to whether Marne would agree. Marne was held to be so very shy and quiet that he might be too embarrassed to talk about himself. So it was agreed that if Marne consented he should be interviewed without a third party being present. Marne agreed to the arrangement and was only too ready to tell his own story.

In a very quiet voice he maintained his willingness to help in any enquiry into the difficulties which middle-aged people like himself might encounter in training. His main drawback had been lack of confidence. He spoke slowly—softly—and sometimes seemed to be searching for words, but what he did say was thoughtful, intelligent and convincing.

His own lack of confidence was a 'personal' problem. To the rejoinder that his own special difficulties were of particular interest, especially as he had now become one of the best all-rounders in the department, he smiled and said slowly, 'Yes, ... I can now operate any of the grinding machines with confidence, but I was not able to do so at the time of the training courses four years ago'.

What had been the precise difficulties? 'Well, ... I was only on the original course for two weeks and this was far too short a time for me to get to grips with it. Even after I made a second start and took a second two weeks, I still could not get the hang of it. I'd had no experience whatever of precision grinding work.' He explained that his previous work on a press machine had been very different. Before this he had been a maintenance worker on machine repair work. His course on precision grinding had allowed far too little time on job practice. 'To my way of looking at it, it was all a matter of practice. I find that I learn by doing—but I am poor at grasping what it is all about when I am instructed—I like to learn by doing the job again and again, and quietly thinking it over.'

His own inhibitions and modesty were not, however, the entire explanation. A more important difficulty was that in the machine shop he had to rely for advice and guidance on the man alongside, who was on production work. 'In the first place he did not have enough time to show me and in the second place he could not explain things very clearly.' The shop supervisor later corroborated this, explaining that the course instructor himself was not always available and was not sufficiently qualified to teach all the details of the job himself.

Marne continued: 'I would try to work alongside the production operator and then I would have to go back to the classroom for an hour. In that time I found that there was not enough time to learn anything properly before I had to go back on the machines again. And so it went on ... And on the practical side as well—you did not have enough time to master the job. I was slow because I was worried by the extent to which I might produce scrap. We had that drummed into us again and again. In every case the answer was that I had produced no scrap. I had however been very slow ... and I continued to be slow even on the second attempt.

'Eventually they put me on a different type of machine— on an "auto-machine" where an assistant was essential. This machine was more like the one I had worked on in the press shop and of course there was an operator in charge. He kept on showing me the job. This gave me a better chance to learn. Also I was there for some months and it is only by practice that you get the real hang of any job.

'After that I went on to my present type of machines where from time to time I was given a different "stand-in" job to do. This gave me a much clearer idea of the general pattern and run of the work. And,' he added very slowly and firmly, 'it also gave me confidence.'

Today, in spite of the pace of the work which has considerably increased, Alfred Marne can confidently tackle work in any part of the shop. Like George Jenkins, he is one of the best and most reliable men in the department. Yet his learning experience had been vastly different.

3. THE OLDER LEARNER IN FORMAL TRAINING

As a 56-year-old process worker with just over twenty years' experience in the chemical industry, John Campbell had been selected, in spite of his age, for work on a new continuous process in the Agricultural Division of I.C.I. Ltd. He was regarded as a little above average on the non-continuous plant which had given him a good working knowledge of the basic skills of the industry. He had learned to control pressure, temperature, level and flow measurement; he had some appreciation of basic chemistry and physics; and his work had often required him to carry out simple calculations.

The new plant, however, demanded a much greater level of theoretical knowledge. A course lasting six weeks had been prepared as a background for later practical training. The first three weeks comprised one week of calculations, one week of physics, and one of chemistry. The second three weeks were devoted to the theoretical aspects of the process, applying some of the basic knowledge gained in the first three weeks.

Because of varying trainee ability and experience, the organizers anticipated problems during the first three weeks. In particular, there were some doubts about how well John Campbell would progress on the course. He had been brought up in a rural community and had left school at 14. After a number of jobs, mainly in farming, he had become a textile worker, then a munitions worker before finally entering the chemical industry. His practical experience seemed reasonable enough, but his lack of education, about which Campbell was himself very conscious, might prove a stumbling block.

When the course started, Campbell seemed to set himself apart from the rest of the group. Although outspoken, he was not normally an aggressive person, yet he frequently lashed out at other course members. In the early stages there was a good deal of freedom to discuss problems. Campbell was reluctant to discuss his difficulties and much more inclined to criticize others. This untypical behaviour isolated him from the rest of the group and made things even more difficult.

The classwork in the first week was mainly calculations and simple mathematics. Campbell's first efforts in this direction were disastrous. By the middle of the second day of the course he decided he had had enough—he just gave up and sat back. He took no active part in the lessons and made no attempt to do the examples set. He asked simply to be ignored and, although putting on a brave front, was clearly distressed.

The tutor was convinced that Campbell's problem was not a lack of ability, and realizing the possible consequences of taking him off the course, decided to leave him where he was, at least for a few days. Gradually Campbell began taking part once more. He refused to tackle the written work, but would join in discussions.

Confidence from previous experience

The first real breakthrough, and the only dramatic turning point, occurred on the fifth day. This was devoted almost entirely to one subject—the use of a slide-rule. Few of the people on the course had ever used a slide-rule before; Campbell had. He was, in fact, fairly proficient and this reversed his position in the group. From being far behind he suddenly found himself in front. The rest of that day was a delight to Campbell and a relief to the course tutor.

When he returned after the weekend to begin a week mainly of physics, his confidence was still visibly increased. Although by no means completely sure of himself, he was at least giving himself the benefit of the doubt.

The practical nature of the physics course appealed to Campbell and served to reinforce his strengthened position. His hostility to the group disappeared and he became more and more active. The third week of chemistry proved difficult for him and he was depressed a little, but to nothing like the extent he had been by the maths.

A test was given at the end of the third week. To Campbell's obvious and genuine amazement he gained a score only a little below the class average. This finally confirmed the suspicion he had that they were not perhaps all that much brighter than he was!

The second half of the course gave Campbell few problems. The practical nature of it appealed to him and his experience of the subject matter (pumps, compressors, instruments, and so on) gave him a positive advantage. Although much of the equipment discussed in this period was new and up to date, the instructors were careful to use the course members' knowledge of simple equipment as a starting point. By using the trainees' experience in this way, older and more experienced people such as Campbell benefited.

He was more able than most to relate the theoretical concepts to the function of the plant equipment and clearly gained much from the course. He achieved a final test score above the group average which, considering his age and academic disadvantages, was very satisfactory. He went on to complete his on-the-job training successfully and become a useful member of a highly skilled process team.

When the training was completed and the strain was over, Campbell was ready to talk about the course as a whole and his reactions to it. To begin with, he had shown a somewhat neutral attitude towards the whole thing, not knowing what to expect. He had been told very little about the course and, with no previous formal training since leaving school, the whole exercise became 'a voyage into the unknown'. At that stage he was not worried about working with younger men— at least not before the course began. His great fears were, as he put it, of 'failing to make the grade', 'being out of my depth', and 'looking daft in front of everybody'.

Campbell had been gratified to find that his knowledge about using a slide-rule had been useful after all, but he sensed that his real recovery came during the physics session. It was then that he began to suspect that some of the younger trainees were not so bright as he had imagined. He had progressed reasonably well during these sessions and he was struck by the thought: 'how nice it was to be doing things and not just listening'. It was tentatively suggested that the examples and problem solving exercises during the maths session were also 'doing things'; not, however, in Campbell's opinion. That was not real 'doing'; whereas he appreciated the 'realism' of the physics sessions and the work on the pump and instruments. He used this term a number of times when comparing the physics and chemistry sessions. In fact, both subjects received similar treatment, with special use being made in the latter of some excellent animated films and visual aids. Nevertheless, in the trainee's view, the physics seemed to be much more 'realistic'. This is not surprising if one takes into account the wealth of experience Campbell had gained from years of work with 'process' machinery and controls. The theories of heat and mechanics could be illustrated in terms of the trainee's experience and more clearly than the abstract concepts of chemistry. As a process operator, Campbell had been concerned with heating, cooling, and transfer of materials rather than the chemistry of a process which remained rather remote and mysterious. It was still not a subject which he felt he grasped.

It seems that in half a life-time of work experience, no matter how filled with myth and factory folk lore, there must be some knowledge on which to base new learning for the elderly trainee. The most unsuitable and thoughtless opening remark an instructor can make to a retraining course, but one still to be heard, is 'I want you to forget all you ever knew about this job—we're going to start from scratch'.

GUIDE TO ACTION

A slow start means that something is amiss. With a single trainee there is the possibility of a poor placement but there is nearly always an additional training reason. When a slow start occurs amongst several trainees at any one time it points axiomatically to some failure in training design, in the comprehension of the nature of the problems which trainees experience at the outset of their training. A slow beginning will become an augury of ultimate failure unless the training officer embarks on some new line of action.

Making training purposeful

Older learners find it difficult to progress unless they see the ultimate purpose of their learning. They are much affected by their conception of what happens at the end of training and by whether a job is being held open for them. If a job is clearly earmarked, it pays to allow the trainees to visit the location and to talk to experienced workmen. This seems to be far more important than mere consideration of the utility of what it is they are ultimately to produce. The end results are seen in highly personal terms and it is only later that interest spreads to the product and the processes that make it. The type of training also bears on its purposefulness. Trainees will relate what they are doing to the job that they have seen or imagine. If they can see no link, due to the protracted or remote nature of preparatory training, interest will rapidly wane. Simplified 'whole' tasks rather than tasks centering on broken-down elements sustain the image of training as a meaningful operation.

Ensuring early comprehension

Trainees are often not clear what is expected of them and, even if they have been told, the message needs to register. There is some experimental evidence to show that written instructions are more effective than spoken and that the reason for this is that they can be referred to at leisure. But comprehension is chiefly a positive process which depends on active conceptualization and involvement rather than in the filling in of points that they have missed. The middle-aged learner should be assisted in building up concepts of the new skill and of how 'it all fits together' by asking him questions and encouraging him to expand on the way he sees things. Conceptualizing may take longer initially than learning by rote, but what is acquired in this way is better retained.

Teaching new terminology

Often the most overwhelming part of a beginner's experience is the new language he has to learn. It is this language which marks out the alien environment in which he finds himself. Yet this learning is of only secondary importance to learning the core of a skill and adjusting to the demands of the work situation. Fixation on the difficulties of the language can be avoided by:

(*a*) letting the beginner learn the language first by working on an ancillary job;
(*b*) offering a handout or booklet which will define the jargon and technical terms (preferably with illustrations) and which he can take home with him if he chooses;
(*c*) playing down the need for learning the language but labelling tools and materials appropriately and making the learning incidental. In this case the instructor will refrain from using the jargon until later.

Developing basic skills

Slow beginners may have to learn or improve basic skills. In manual work, handling technique may have a special importance; in machine shop work it may be familiarity with machine controls, instrument reading or micrometer measurement; in other pursuits it may be arithmetic or systematic note-taking. Some basic skills are assumed in almost every course of training. Unless these skills are checked in a tactful way at the outset, and compensatory measures taken where necessary, unforeseen difficulties may arise.

Unblocking

Older 'listeners' tend to lose the track of a course when they meet a particular point which they feel impelled to relate, whether openly or silently, to their own experience. They miss a good deal by the time they switch on again and find the subject has changed. The slow beginner may then forget what he has already learned and feel obliged to start all over again.

Sudden changes in topic and theme must be avoided. Experiments have shown that as age increases, the learning of new material also tends to interfere with the consolidation of what has been learned recently. These interferences are among the chief causes of blockage in memorization in middle and later life. They also show themselves as the adverse consequences of distractions. Adults suffer more than youngsters from distraction caused by external worries and strains during learning, and these sources of disturbance outside training may severely limit progress.

Adult trainees should be dissuaded from taking on too much at once, from coping with a change of house, new schools and so on, while at the same time learning a new job.

In addition, wherever possible, training should be planned in an environment free from stress and interruption.

Understanding and help with personal problems at work *and* home are responsibilities which the instructor should be ready to undertake.

5. Social Relationships

INTRODUCTION: THE INDIVIDUAL AND HIS GROUP

Inevitably, when managers think of training they direct their thoughts towards the more tangible, more visible features—the equipment and materials, the schedules and the documentary work, all of which provide some solid grounds for the assessment of efficiency. But the views which trainees form of their training are likely to be dominated by reactions to colleagues, supervisors, and the general atmosphere and environment in which the training takes place. When the die is cast, the trainee—like the proverbial customer—is always right, for the dissatisfied trainee will end up by taking his custom elsewhere. This he does by dropping out, either during the course of training or following transfer to the actual work situation for which he has been inadequately prepared.

The relationship between the individual and his group becomes as important as his aptitude for learning in affecting his chances of surviving the course and his results at the end of it.

This chapter describes a number of industrial training programmes in which the results achieved escape any convincing explanation other than that of the climate and atmosphere in which the training was conducted. A company short of full-time coil winders was reluctant to engage available older applicants because, they said, trainability on coil winding operations declines steeply with age (a contention well supported by one industrial study). Yet, paradoxically, it transpires that older women were being trained for the job on an evening shift. These evening shift workers overcame their natural handicaps and surpassed all reasonable expectations by out-performing day workers. Why?

A second case study poses some similar questions about the relationship between individual performance and the group situation. Two community action programmes are set up within striking distance of one another in the U.S.A. The objective of each is to reduce the substantial numbers of unemployed and 'unemployables' within their city centres by recruiting, training and upgrading them. The operation is well supported financially in both cases. Yet one achieves such meagre results that many doubt if it was worthwhile. The other is so successful that it becomes not only a model in the U.S.A. but achieves some international fame. Anyone scanning the progress of each might be persuaded that in one scheme the target population behaved in a 'disappointing' way while in the other they proved pliant and responsive. Yet why should populations react so differently in apparently similar circumstances?

The third case study takes place in one of the valleys of South Wales. A factory in the motor trade has built up a strong position in a highly competitive industry. The work people are overwhelmingly in the middle or later years of life, they have all been retrained for their current work at a much higher age than is normal in training, and they are all chronically sick men, victims of pneumoconiosis who have retired from or have been invalided out of mining. A success story in the face of great physical disadvantage is usually a mark of the triumphant human spirit, of the boundless possibilities that spring from high morale. So it appears to be with these ex-miners. They learn not one job, but several; they move between semi-skilled and skilled work to meet production demands with a versatility and panache that belies the recency of their second careers. From first to last they are buddies, mates, comrades. Is this the essential, elusive something of which we can all too easily lose sight in training and management?

1. THE SUCCESSFUL EVENING SHIFT

Shortly after World War II, a company was established which introduced lighter work into an area of declining heavy industry. The initial total labour force of 600 had grown over two decades to 2,500. In the early days there were plenty of young applicants for jobs and it was natural to adopt a policy of selecting only young people for those operations which required the greatest expenditure of time, money, and care in training. One such operation was coil winding.

In this particular firm, the operation involved the winding of wire of about the thickness of a human hair on to cores ranging from $\frac{1}{2}$ in. to 3 in. (12-75 mm, approx.) long. Two types of winding machine were in use, a single-head machine operating at up to 6,000 r.p.m. and a double-headed type running up to 10,000 r.p.m. Both worked on a principle similar to the shuttle filling mechanism of a domestic sewing machine. Operating either type constituted a sedentary occupation, a factor which should have commended them to older workers. However, because of a philosophy that casts doubt on the suitability of older trainees for coil winding—it is often said that there is a rapid deterioration of ability to learn this skill after the early 20s—the company tended to recruit older women only for the less skilled jobs in spite of a comparative shortage of younger women applicants.

For some time, an evening shift had been employed in the coil winding department, following a need to increase production without buying more machines and using up further space. While it was company policy to seek younger applicants for the full-time day shift, a high proportion of applicants for the evening shift were middle-aged, mainly women whose families no longer required their full-time care and who were keen to get back into employment. So the recognition of realities paved the way for a more liberal employment policy. During a period of one year, more than 80 per cent of those engaged for coil winding on the evening shift were over 25 years old, and about 40 per cent were between 35 and 51 years.

The formal training procedure for all coil winders was based on skills analysis. There were preliminary exercises in handling the machine and the materials, but the aim was to start the trainee actually winding coils at the earliest possible moment. She was encouraged to set her own targets. After noting the time taken to wind one coil, she would try to improve on this with each successive attempt. Then she would endeavour to reduce the time taken to complete a set. Normally, trainees are said to be capable of producing coils during the fourth week but require 12-14 weeks to reach experienced worker standard. All trainees remained in the training section until they were able to produce good coils in the basic time allowance of five minutes per coil. Thereafter they were closely followed up by the instructor with the production target set at $2\frac{1}{2}$ minutes per coil.

During the one year period under review there were fifty-five women trained on the day shift, having a median age of 19 years and ranging from 15 to 33 years. In the same period, fifty-six women were trained on the evening shift, where the median age was 32 years with a range from 20 to 51 years. An analysis of the training results showed that in spite of the higher age of the evening shift recruits, 93 per cent succeeded in completing their training, compared with 87 per cent of the day shift.

Good results by evening shift

Because of their increased age, the evening shift trainees might have been expected to have poorer results. Could this reversal be accounted for by differences in the length of training? Management often allows for the fact that older recruits take longer to train than younger people. But the facts hardly showed any differences in the length of time required by the two shifts to learn this skill, i.e. to maintain winding performance at five minutes per coil. Both shifts required a median training time of 180 hours using the single-headed machine, and on the double-head winder, the evening shift needed only 160 hours compared with the day shift's 200.

The older trainees also compared favourably in other ways. After the training period had been completed, the production per man hour from the older coil winders on the evening shift was equal to that of the day shift. Labour turnover of the new evening shift members after training also compared favourably with that of their younger day shift colleagues. Three months after completion of training, 82 per cent of the evening shift trainees were still employed and only 66 per cent of the day shift; twelve months later, the figures were 57 per cent and 40 per cent, while two years after training, 50 per cent of the evening shift trainees were still employed, and only 22 per cent of the day shift. The relatively high survival rate of the older trainees endorses the earlier indication that coil winding is a suitable operation for older workers once the skills have been acquired. Thus the older trainees proved equal or superior to the younger women in terms of training time, productivity, and labour turnover, whereas the reverse might commonly have been expected. This could not be accounted for by differences in training procedure between the two groups. Both used the same machines in a corner of the production shop, the same training method, a similar trainee:instructor ratio, and even the same instructors.

Possible explanations

Were there circumstantial differences which might account for the better result on the evening shift? One factor to consider is the length of the daily training period. The evening shift workers inevitably had shorter spells of learning than those on the day shift. For a demanding manual skill this is usually an advantage in offsetting the destructive influence of fatigue. On the other hand, older recruits tend in general to appreciate long rather than short training sessions. These two points might seem to cancel one another out.

A second possibility in the relatively superior performance of the evening shift recruits lies in a common belief that evening shift applicants in general are a special group strongly motivated and of a higher calibre than the average full-time applicant for industrial employment. The company's selection test results however showed no reason to believe that the evening shift workers were more gifted.

The main reasons which evening shift applicants give for seeking work are social or economic—to be better able to raise the young families that preclude them from working during the day, and to earn money for 'extras'. These, however, are also the motives of many older full-time applicants whose families are at work all day, or who are striving to keep teen-age children at school and college. But evening shift opportunities tend to be restricted to manufacturing operations, and it is therefore supposed that women capable of more responsible work may have no choice but to accept evening employment in factories.

Calmer evening atmosphere

A third and obvious difference relates to the time of day in which learning takes place. It could be assumed that because an evening shift trainee had already completed one day's work —be it housework or duties of another kind—she would be too fatigued for a second session, especially if concentrated learning was required. However, there is usually the minimum number of service, technical, and advisory personnel on duty in the evening, and it is customary to solve problems and initiate necessary changes during the day shift so that work can proceed on an evening shift as smoothly as possible. Thus a calmer atmosphere is likely to prevail in the evening. and both common sense and the results of experimental work suggest that this should assist the older trainees. Such an atmosphere would also provide the background for the formation of social groups. A middle-aged woman has little interest in the general conversation between teenage girls at work; yet conversation with other people outside her own family is often one of the motivating reasons for returning to employment. The evening shift trainees had in common their family responsibilities and their endeavour to resume a type of employment for which they required training.

It is not only during the learning period that 'climate' is important. Other studies have shown that the first few months after completion of training tend to be even more critical for older people than for young. Their long-term survival in the job depends a great deal on the reception which they get from line supervision and colleagues whilst they are becoming experienced at the job they have learned. In this case, the evening shift trainees survived the period of transition and adjustment to the production situation better than the day shift; in fact, those who stayed longest were those in the highest age groups of the evening shift.

The most convincing explanation of the superior results on the evening shift came from the factory grape-vine. There was a 'better spirit' on the evening shift. The line supervision seemed to carry out their responsibilities for 'settling in' trainees more diligently than on the day shift. Relieved of some of the stress of the day shift situation, foremen and chargehands devoted more time to the encouragement, praise and, where necessary, the constructive criticism of new members on the line. This made the trainee feel that her continued progress mattered just as much as it did whilst she was one of a much smaller group in the training section. It would also seem to have had a greater effect upon the older trainees than the younger. This period is the critical testing time of self-confidence and self-esteem. If older trainees win through they tend to stay with the job.

There is scattered evidence from other industries about older women trained for an evening shift who have later transferred to the day shift. They too have continued in full-time employment for worthwhile periods of time and their performance on the day shift has been maintained at a satisfactory level. Skills and work habits have an impressive stability once they have been able to form in a satisfactory environment.

2. COMMUNITY ACTION PROGRAMS IN THE U.S.A.

This section offers a comparison and contrast between experiences in two towns, Bridgeport and New Haven, in a single state of the U.S.A. The occasion for crossing the Atlantic, in our description of human reactions to retraining, springs from the involvement of one of the authors in the project at New Haven as consultant on loan to the U.S. Department of Labor.

Bridgeport is a smoky town in Connecticut dominated by a number of engineering companies and containing both prosperous areas and run-down suburbs housing the poor and the workless. Although unemployment was high, the employment prospects appeared brighter than in most depressed areas. The town's industries were booming and there were very many vacancies for skilled and semi-skilled workers. But the impediment to jobs-for-all lay in the fact that the workless were mostly of poor education and lacking in the skills and experience demanded by Bridgeport's industries.

'Community action program' is the term used in the U.S.A. to describe projects aimed at revitalizing depressed areas by direct action in stimulating employment and tackling social problems. These projects operate on a typically American pattern. They depend on funds from both public and private sources, they are sponsored jointly by federal and local government, and yet each remains autonomous and independent. There is no standard approach. In the case of Bridgeport, much of the starting initiative had come from the State of Connecticut. The target group for the programme was the 12,000 unemployed. The intention was to develop a means of assisting them to secure employment in the town's growing industries through a retraining programme conducted in special workshops.

Selecting trainees for jobs

Initially, 4,400 job applicants were screened, and of these about 1,500 were interviewed. Nearly one-third of the interviewees were rejected as unsuitable and almost another third were not interested. The remaining 600 were recommended for testing by the United States Employment Service. The whittling process went on: 200 did not appear for tests and another 250 failed the tests. Of the 150 who passed the selection tests, 66 either failed to start training or dropped out during the first week, or for some other reason failed to finish the course. Ultimately, of the original 4,400 applicants, only 84 completed the training. The eventual effect both on the unemployed and on the filling of job vacancies in the town's industries was only marginal.

There is only scanty information to suggest how it was that a grandly conceived scheme should produce so puny a result. Perhaps the whole project had been guided by the logic of the 'economic man'. On financial grounds, the jobs available offered an 'incentive' for the workless whatever level of welfare benefits they were receiving. The mechanism of this community action plan suggested that the guiding purpose was to slot people into the vacant jobs by providing certain essential facilities, and it was to be expected that the workless would take full advantage of the facilities provided. But it was the response of people to these opportunities that proved disappointing. They did not behave in a way that seemed sensible, grateful or in their own interest and the intended participants became the object of a good deal of unfavourable comment. But what would have happened if there had been fewer ready-made assumptions about the target population? The workless had not been the subject of any real study, and the notions of what was needed to get them back into employment had been oversimplified.

Several American studies have built up a very full picture

of the characteristics of the long-term unemployed.* A history of rebuffs tends to make the unemployed very apathetic about job-seeking. They hold exaggerated beliefs about their inadequacies and the prejudices against them (whether on account of colour or age). They are ill-informed about the opportunities that do exist and such applications that they make for jobs depend almost entirely on personal contacts. As a group, they are singularly ill-prepared to make the most of their assets and to use whatever resources are available. Any programme which fails to take this into account is liable to run into difficulties.

Creating jobs and manpower

Two stops down the railroad from Bridgeport is New Haven which set up at about the same time a community action program under the name of Community Progress Inc. CPI is a notable institution in that the Mayor of the city, Mark Lee, and the Executive Director, Mitchell Sviridoff, succeeded in bringing together the various agencies that were operating in welfare work and state relief into a single co-ordinating and administrative body. The policy of CPI was to combine 'urban renewal and human renewal'. This made it possible to replan the slum areas of the city, to encourage new enterprises to establish themselves, to rehouse part of the displaced population and to provide all the services the workless needed to enable them to obtain regular employment. Many of the interface problems usually found in these separate areas of activity were overcome since CPI was an all-embracing organization minimally concerned with inter-departmental boundaries. Additionally, it was subject to the personal influence of the Mayor who in American politics has far greater powers in decision-making on city matters than his equivalent on the British scene.

During the immediate post-war years, New Haven had all

---

* Wilcock, R. C. and Franke, W. H. *Unwanted Workers*. London: Free Press of Glencoe, 1963.

the ingredients of the typical American troubled city. A large central semi-slum area housed a predominantly Negro and Puerto-Rican population, densely packed, underemployed and with a disproportionately high rate of crime and alcoholism. The ever-present vicious circle obstructed remedies: rehousing would mean larger rents which in turn demanded higher incomes; these incomes would need to come from better than-menial-jobs which would be available only for those of adequate skill and educational status; this meant up-grading a population that identified itself with the rotting city scene.

The city authorities took vigorous steps to improve employment opportunities. Favourable building sites were offered to companies expanding employment. Officers, called Job Developers, were appointed to explore the job potentialities of established firms. They paid personal visits to companies to discuss what jobs might become available if the right type of skilled labour could be found. In some cases where an employer did not believe that a vacancy was likely to be filled, he had withheld notification of it. In other cases, the job developer would persuade an employer that it was worth creating a job in some area of the company's activities that seemed to justify expansion.

In this way, Community Progress Inc. carried out an intimate study of the job market while at the same time succeeding in expanding the number of jobs. The next task was to develop the manpower to match the jobs. It was here that fundamental obstacles were seen. The workless lacked occupational skills and were regarded as being poor in educability and trainability. Moreover, experience had shown that it was not simply a matter of providing opportunity. Those who had been long out of work were reluctant to pursue openings because they had no faith that they would gain a stable job at the end. To some extent this prophecy was self-fulfilling. Being generally unmotivated, the conduct, discipline, and punctuality of those who had been taken into a limited programme fell a good deal short of that which was desirable and acceptable. In essence the problem was that the workless in-

cluded a solid core of people commonly described as 'unemployables', while the biggest group would normally have been
regarded as marginals (most had one drawback or another).

Approaching potential trainees

The imaginative approach was to make the starting point of
contact the street or the home. A number of neighbourhood
workers were enrolled and were assigned the task of seeking
personal interviews with the unemployed and endeavouring
ultimately to enlist their interest in some of the services that
CPI provided. The neighbourhood worker always resided in
his allotted quarter of the city and in some cases already had
a large network of acquaintances extending into the rougher
areas. A typical first contact might result in an invited visit to
the home. Inspection of a housing problem would encourage
contact with one of the project's welfare workers, termed
'homemakers', who might in due course help the wife with
some of her budgeting problems. After confidence had been
built up, the householder would be encouraged to enrol with
one of the adult work training programs.

But a 'problem recruit' would seldom be given immediate
access to the more advanced courses. Instead, he would be persuaded to 'take a job' temporarily with a work crew program.
These work crews consisted of teams of people who worked
on simple assignments, such as erecting fencing for the local
hospital or painting the bays in the municipal bus garage.
Each crew was led by a hardworking practitioner who had at
the same time experience and knowledge of social work. The
prime objective was to develop self-respect, to learn the meaning of team work and to accord with the demands for punctuality and discipline which regular work imposes. The work
crew proved especially valuable for two groups, first for the
younger people for whom the crew leader often provided a
father image that helped them to establish their own identity,
and secondly, for the recruits with a psychiatric history or a
background of general disturbance.

The main aim of the project, of course, was to upgrade the individual by training him in a skill. Some of the recruits would hear of the training offered and would be attracted into the scheme by the desire to learn a given trade. Others would be transferred from a work crew when the work crew leader judged it would be most timely for their development. Ultimately, all those enrolled found themselves being trained for one of the special occupational skills. Yet while specialization was encouraged, over-specialization was discouraged. Each trainee spent a proportion of his time undergoing a short course in the other skills offered in the training centre. For example, someone being trained as a data processing operator would also work on machine shop work and electrical training as additional subjects. For others, these would be their special areas. Extending the opportunity to learn briefly about other skills increased a trainee's eventual scope and mitigated disappointment if he was finally placed in a job outside his special area of training.

Additional services

CPI offered still further services. A counsellor was available for trainees who required his help. This counsellor would assist mainly in advising those who suffered some marked employment disability, usually for medical reasons, or whose personal problems interfered with their progress and prospects. Finally, all trainees enjoyed the benefits of a sophisticated placement service which attempted to match realistically the demands of the job with the abilities and personal characteristics of the man. The fortunes of CPI rested squarely on its local reputation. Responsibilities had to be discharged to the trainees, but the wish to make a job placement could not be allowed to endanger the confidence that had been built up with local employers. Making a placement was therefore a delicate operation demanding equal service to both parties.

By now it must be apparent that the community action program at New Haven differed from that in neighbouring

Bridgeport in several important aspects. The Bridgeport program was concerned with jobs and employment and offered a useful range of amenities. But the facilities were not available to all. The high emphasis placed on selection made it plain that the basic intention was to skim the cream of the unemployed to fill some of the outstanding vacancies. As a plan, it failed to capture the imagination of the local community or lost it at some point along the line so that its final effects were marginal.

The community action program at New Haven on the other hand was people-centred from the outset. The concept of 'human renewal' was regarded as the essential counterpart to urban renewal. It was the resolution to solve the human problems, whatever they were, that lay at the heart of the imaginatively conceived manpower program which Mitchell Sviridoff, the former Executive Director of CPI, has depicted in the following terms:

'There are lots of ways of evaluating New Haven's manpower program. One is by using numbers and percentages, and they are impressive. But even more important is that for the first time we have created an interlocking network of systems that assures that the person who needs help will end up in a training program and will end up in a job. And it will be more than just a job. In the great majority of cases it will be the right job, and one with a potential for growth and advancement. Jobs that just pass the time of day and lead nowhere are not part of the New Haven program.

'What CPI and its allies have done is to fashion a true employment system that covers every area of need and every stage of preparation for, placement in, and effective performance on, a job. We have taken scattered elements and pulled them together into an integrated group of systems that guarantees maximum return to the person who needs help and to the public and private agencies that underwrite our program.'

Some statistics are useful in putting Sviridoff's claim into perspective. New Haven has a population of about 150,000 people. During 2½ years operation of the manpower program, 3,841 people were trained and placed in jobs. These jobs represented advancement in a very real way, for those who were placed in new jobs received an average of 25 per cent higher earnings than in any job previously held. The unemployment rate of the city, once notoriously high, was brought in a few years below the national average.

What statistics do not reveal so easily is that the manpower program, rather than concentrating on those who were easy to place, went out of its way to bring back into worthwhile employment those who had fallen by the wayside.

Take the case of Bob who at the age of 21 had never worked. He had a long history of emotional problems and involvement with the police. For two years he had been a patient at a psychiatric clinic and was much subject to lapses into alcoholism. When first drawn into the manpower program he was placed in a work crew operating in a city park. After a period of help from a counselling psychologist and further training, he was placed in a job as a mill hand. He has since written to his helpers expressing his gratitude and thanks.

Al was a 30 year old, quiet, studious, lanky negro who performed proficiently in the data processing classes. It was not surprising that when the regular instructor left he was invited to take his place. What was surprising, however, was that he had originally come into the manpower program as a misfit who, though a good machinist, had been unable to find a job. He advanced from a work crew program to an intermediate program and eventually was placed in a job at a library. But he came back for more and presented himself for training in data processing. Eventually he relinquished his job as Instructor, went on a two-week course run by International Business Machines and was last heard of in a supervisory job in an electronics factory.

But none was more remarkable than George, a 40 year old white patient who was recruited on discharge from a local hospital. An unsuccessful marriage and a failure in business had preceded his attempt at suicide by driving into the abutments of a bridge. He had remained seriously ill for eighteen months and even on final discharge he was left completely paralysed in both arms and legs.

George was not only physically handicapped but severely disturbed. He was referred to the counselling psychologist who was able to help him with a number of his personal problems starting with the termination of an unhappy marriage. After obtaining his divorce, George was able to regain his self-respect and develop a positive interest in life. In due course it became apparent that George had a great capacity for projecting his personality. His counsellor continued to assist him over a period and finally found him a job as a licensed securities representative, a job which could be performed largely on the telephone. George not only held the job but achieved distinction in it. First he won a competitive sales award from his nation-wide investment securities firm for outstanding sales achievement, and then a little later he was promoted to district manager in a local area office.

The manpower program at New Haven outstripped all provisional forecasts. The state employment service had predicted an ultimate placement rate of not more than 20 per cent of those who had been enrolled in the training programme. In fact over 75 per cent of the trainees completing their training were placed in suitable employment and three months later 70 per cent were still in the same job. The difference between the predicted and actual result revolved round a human question. It was a matter of how far the trainees would respond to their training and how lasting the response would be. For once, the capacity of the workless to better themselves had been underestimated.

3. MINERS ON FACTORY PRODUCTION

The British Leyland factory at Bargoed in South Wales was

established in 1949 as part of the former Austin Motor Company. The name Austin still stands on the plinth above the front door, in spite of a number of mergers—the Austin Motor Company, the British Motor Corporation, British Motor Holdings and British Leyland (Austin-Morris) Ltd. The latest title is bestowed on the large hoarding at the front of the grounds. But to the local population it is immaterial. They continue to refer to the factory by the earlier and more intimate name of 'Austin's'.

There would be nothing remarkable about the factory were it not for the fact that it is, and always has been, staffed entirely by workers—mostly elderly—suffering from pneumonoconiosis. Ex-miners must have been a welcome new addition to the work force at a time when labour was scarce, but the motive in restricting recruitment *entirely* to victims of 'the chest' from the surrounding coal-mining area can only have been philanthropic. There is a continuous trickle of fit and younger men who regularly present themselves for jobs at the factory, but they are turned away.

For all that, the factory makes no claims on charity. It is true that the Government makes an allowance of fifty per cent of the rent. This is normal for a factory which has more than twelve per cent of the workers disabled. But there is no special dispensation for having 100 per cent employees disabled and there are no hidden subsidies. The factory accounts were originally merged with those of the parent company's but now the Bargoed factory is for most practical purposes independent and operates according to the normal commercial criteria. Costs, quality and delivery times are all-important and on all three the reputation of the factory is high. There is no shrinking from the hurly-burly of the motor industry. The competitive position of Bargoed is revealed, usually most favourably, whenever small- to medium-sized contracts normally undertaken there are put out to tender.

What is it that makes this factory so successful? There is nothing very unusual about its general system of operation, but all its features underline versatility and team spirit and its record shows accomplishment in the way it overcomes its problems.

There are two shifts: 250 men work on the 8 a.m.—4.30 p.m. day shift, and 150 men on the night shift, which involves 10 p.m.—7.30 a.m. for four nights and 5 p.m.—9 p.m. for one night. All men receive a shop- and a supplementary-bonus based on production at the main Longbridge factory. There are no individual piece rates. All the men belong to a single union—the Amalgamated Engineering Federation. There are no demarcation limits anywhere in the factory, although there are three grades of pay according to the skills that have been acquired. A man receives his rate of pay even if management wishes him to transfer for a while to a less skilled job, so he can be on maintenance on one day but cleaning-up the next. Although the factory is making a variety of motor components and contains a range of large modern presses, there is only one tradesman who has learned his skill outside—an electrician.

Versatility is a very useful quality in the motor industry with its frequent fluctuations in production. It is often possible at Bargoed to switch from one motor component to another, but the really useful standby is the 'joy car', which the company had once planned to have as its main product. This is a model Austin car which can be pedal-driven by young children and is often seen adorning the showroom of the Austin dealer. When times are slack, workers are switched to the 'joy car', but when the motor trade is booming, production of the model is lessened.

Training plays an important part in helping to create a versatile labour force. Every new employee receives eight hours induction training. He may work on assembly which is allotted sixteen or twenty-four hours training according to the operation. There are many opportunities for the further development of personal skill through training; for example, to work in the trim shop involves a further 91 hours training, in inspection another 160 hours, progress needs 164 hours and maintenance no less than 572 hours.

Easy adjustment to factory life

The older miners adapt to factory life at Bargoed with remarkable ease. It is this capacity for adjustment which stands out at the factory as its most singular feature. From conversation at all levels, the men appear co-operative, and grateful for all that has been done for them. This contention gains support also from the statistics. In spite of their age, ill-health and their proneness to absence in January and February when respiratory complaints are at their worst, their overall absenteeism for the year stands about the same as that for the engineering industry as a whole. Labour turnover is slightly higher than average but can be accounted for mainly by retirement and death, due of course to the unusual age structure of the factory. During the last year, only seven out of 450 employees left of their own accord, most of these due to special circumstances.

ITRU was given the opportunity to talk with a random sample of the men. Below we offer the transcripts, slightly abbreviated. The men have ordinary stories to tell. Less ordinary are their attitudes.

Hywel Davies, a skilled and highly regarded inspector in the factory, is 58 years old but has only spent two years at Austins.
Before you came here, had you done anything other than mining?
HD: No, I came out of the colliery at 35. I took a clerical course and worked in a builder's office. Then I left to work in a wholesaler's as head clerk. I worked at this for six months, but owing to my health I had to give that up and I was very kindly given a position here.
Was the health problem pneumonoconiosis?
HD: Yes. The strain of working outside in a yard was too great. I went to two specialists. One told me to give up work; the other told me I could carry on if I took lighter work. But it was a nervous breakdown that

brought matters to a head. I was told I had been forcing myself too much and to take life more easily. I think it was because I hadn't had a background in the industry and I was competing with people who had been in an office all their lives.

Didn't you have the same problem here?

HD: No. The manager of this factory accepted me very differently from any other manager. I felt at home and was told to bring any problems to him. I did have trouble with 'nights' and went to him and he put me on day shifts. When I went on the line I was shown what to do. I think I could have got along a little quicker, but he was so patient with me. I was put at my ease all the time.

Is the work in this factory different from any you had previously experienced?

HD: Yes. I had to start all over again, but I was quite happy, because I knew there was not much else I could do.

Did you know any people in the factory before you started?

HD: I worked with a few of the people here twenty years ago.

What training have you received?

HD: Production training—I was trained on trim, then I went to press and then inspection.

How did you react to all these experiences of training?

HD: I found people very kind in the way they treated me and I responded very easily to the treatment.

I get the impression of a very relaxed atmosphere in comparison with a lot of establishments.

HD: Oh yes. At other establishments where I've been, if you didn't succeed you were pushed out. Although I hadn't had the basic training, I had to come up to their standard in such a short time that I was fighting my way along all the time. But here, it was just like walking into a job I had done previously, because not too much was expected of me.

But if things seem so much easier here, how do you account for the efficiency of the factory?

HD: I think it is because workers are absorbed better. Also the supervisors here are more tolerant than elsewhere.

Is this because the supervisors are themselves disabled, and therefore aware of the problems?

Manager (intervening):

No. Hywel Davies' particular supervisor came from Longbridge. We hand-pick our supervisors and look for this quality. We're very careful about their selection. We look not only at their skill on a job, but whether they have other qualities such as understanding.

HD: The supervisor takes you under his wing and really looks after you. Here people know you are a 'dust' victim and you are treated as such. Outside, you tried to hide the fact. You were constantly competing with others while not feeling well.

How does training compare here with elsewhere?

HD: Most favourably. In my other jobs they expected you to act as if you were already experienced. It was a far better training here and they didn't make any expectations. They just wanted you to become more familiar with things and were ready to give you more help if you needed it.

Have you learned a lot on inspection?

HD: Yes. I have enjoyed it, too.

Billy Griffith is 48 years old and had been in the factory for five years, coming straight from the mines.

How did you view the switch coming from mine to factory?

BG: I had never worked in a factory and I was afraid of the change. I thought I wouldn't be able to do anything in a factory. I couldn't imagine what the work would be like.

Did you know people already here?

BG: Yes, but I had never discussed it with them.

How long did your feeling of unease last?

BG: About three weeks—until the end of training. Then I felt much more at home.

Were things different from what you expected?

BG: Oh yes, everything was so technical. The machines do everything for you.

You've now been through several training programmes here. How have you reacted to them?

BG: I've found them perfectly all right. I was not worried and quite enjoyed them. It's better than being in a particular job for every day, week, and year. You're having a variation. You can learn all the time here. I think everyone should have training. It's such a long time before you can find everything out the hard way. If you have a training you can go straight to it. It took us twelve months in our day to find some things out in the mines. If we'd have had training we'd have known that in the beginning.

Did you ever have the feeling that you were too old to learn, and so disliked training?

BG: No.

Is that because you felt settled in the factory at the time?

BG: Yes, but also because I had been here for six months beforehand. I was doing 'nights' then, and that didn't agree with me at all, because I wasn't used to them. I couldn't do 'days' though, because I have four children and the money wasn't good enough. So I went back to the mines until the children were out of the way and then I came back here. So I was prepared to take the drop in money.

Leaving aside the question of money, some people say they would prefer to work in the mines. Would you?

BG: Good gosh no! No, never. I wish I'd never seen the mines. When one of our pits closed I went all round the country with my brother looking for a pit to work at. We thought we could never do such a thing as to work in a factory. We thought factory work was too technical and that the wages of an unskilled person were too low.

I never had a chance to learn a skill unless I went to night school. My father pleaded with my three brothers and me not to go down the pit. But once one boy went down the pit, it was too tempting to the rest of us because the money was so much better than we were earning. We couldn't work in a factory then because there weren't any, so the choice was the pit or a shop.

Was it your disability that brought you into a factory?

BG: Yes. I wouldn't have come in otherwise. I didn't know what opportunities were offered. There is always something to learn here because you are getting different jobs all the time and you have to vary your technique.

Evan Thomas is 53 years old. He worked underground for twenty-seven years, passing through a mining school, becoming an overman and then an economy officer for four collieries (reclaiming timber, rings etc. so that they can be made usable again). On leaving the mines due to the 'dust' he became a steward at a club in the Mumbles and then a publican at a hotel at Aberfan. He has been in Austins for the past two years.

Did you find any difficulty with the work here in a factory?

ET: No. This assembly work is like the work I did in clerical jobs. If you've held a pen in your hand then you can hold some assembly parts in your hand. It's different from holding, say, a pick.

Have you noticed others having difficulties on joining?

ET: For those who had been underground all their lives, eyesight seems a bit of a problem at first on assembly work. But they get used to it in about two weeks and have no more bother. But there are no great difficulties. What's different here is the conditions. You're using your hands all the time. In the mines your legs used to do all the work. Underground, we had ten minutes for food. Ate it where you happened to be. Here you have time to feed *and* digest it. But a lot of people don't like long breaks for feeding. We'd rather get home earlier. In the mines we'd finish at 2 p.m. but here not till 4.30 p.m. It's difficult to get used to the different hours.

(Mainly because of the reason stated here, the men have half an hour only for meals and leave work at 4.30 p.m.)

You say there are no great difficulties. How is it that you find the change to life here so easy?

ET: We all work together. We all help each other. We have the same 'language'—it's underground talk. It doesn't make any difference what colliery a man comes from, you are at home if you are working with him as soon as you start because *he* has been a miner too. All the chaps here will help you out when you're learning. If you've had a bad day, everyone helps you to get your work done. It's the same in the home. If the wife is ill another miner's wife will come in and do the washing and cook the meals so I can come out to work. And if I'm ill, then all my mates will each do a few more assembly jobs to help me out.

Dai Jones, aged 53, spent twenty years as a miner, then went to work on the Treforest industrial estate as a labourer.

Did you worry about working on the large presses when you started?

DJ: No. Machines did not worry me—we had machines in the mines.

Did you know any of the people here at Bargoed?

DJ: Yes. One chap kept saying: 'Why don't you come over to us?' And when my factory had a redundancy, I did.

Was there any difference between being a 'new boy' here and in your Treforest factory?

DJ: When I went to the Treforest factory I was the only one to join them from the mines. I was a bit lost. I was not exactly afraid but the system was so different. But *here* you have worked with *someone* before.

When you work at the pit, three or four of us would always wait for each other to go home—we had done

it for years. But at the Treforest factory, nobody waits
for you—you just go off to catch the bus. You just clock
out and join a bus queue.

I often felt like leaving the other factory and going
back to the pit.

It's very different here. I think there might be one or
two who want to get back to the pit. When there was
a four-day week, two or three went back. In the pit,
everything is in your own hands—responsibility—if
you want it done you have to do it. Every man has to
think for himself in the pit. You only see the boss about
twice a day. So the miner must have a lot of self discipline. Most of the day to day problems you have to solve
for yourself.

You don't have people standing over you here, but
they are there if you want them. It's not just your workmates who have been down the mine with you, it's your
supervisors too.

Thomas Owens, aged 57, is a supervisor, and trains the men
on his section. He spent thirty-eight years in the pit before
starting at the factory. Many trainees have now passed through
his hands.

Who do you find difficult to train?

TO: No-one really—it's not age, it's not the jobs they've had
—it's just personality in the same way as it was in the
mines.

How did you feel when you first started factory work?

TO: I had a feeling of apprehension when I found I was
coming here—a feeling that I might not fit in to any
other job.

I had this feeling until I came in on the first day and
then as soon as I walked in here, it was all wiped away
at once. I knew a majority of the men.

They were all helpful—they pointed things out—
they made things easier. It's home from home—they are
all ex-miners.

Now I train the other men—first they have an induction course—then they come to me and I do the same sort of induction on a smaller scale and make them feel at home. I can't really say that any of my mates had problems. If you can afford to spend the time with them initially, it pays you.

Training? Well I show them that I'm interested in their well-being as well as in their progress in training —and I'm sure that the sooner they feel at home, the sooner we get more work out of them.

Would you go back to the mines?

TO: Gosh! No fear. I'll tell you—I've not told anyone this before, but it's true—I used to dread to get up in the mornings, because I hated to go to the mines. It's so different here, you just can't explain. You feel you get up and dress willingly to come here.

In the mines, I began to feel I just could not cope. After thirty-eight years in the pits, I'd got to an age where you know on the one hand what it's doing to you and your health, and on the other you know you're too old to get another job. It's a great satisfaction to know that you are capable of doing a new type of job.

I began to get miserable and my family said: 'You *must* leave the pit'. I said: 'Don't be silly—where would *I* get another job—I can't leave the pit till I've seen my three daughters married and looked after'. Now where could I get a job at my age? And I had no qualifications.

Then I went to the doctor—and he said the same thing. Then he *made* me make the break. The doctor gave me an introduction to Austins. I'd never thought of it as a possibility of somewhere *I* could go.

He *made* me apply. Now I'm only sorry I'd not done it years ago. I'm sure not a single one would want to go back. Where else would men of our age get a job and be treated like this? This makes us go on working as long as we possibly can.

'Where else would men of our age get a job and be treated

like this?' That question of Thomas Owens would seem the clue to the achievements of a factory staffed by the chronically sick and trained for unfamiliar and often highly technical work, especially in tool-setting and maintenance, in the middle and later years of working life. In spite of their physical handicaps and lack of experience, the men more than hold their own in a strongly competitive industry. The spirit of their community rather than the technical excellence of the training methods provides the foundation of Bargoed's success.

GUIDE TO ACTION

High morale in a group is so infectious that it soon passes to new trainees. In a working environment where people are very much a community and where most members have recent experience of training, the process of learning receives social support and people help one another to overcome difficulties and problems in adjustment. The social environment is capable of depressing or elevating the technical worth of any training programme that is introduced. How can this favourable social climate be created?

Promoting group cohesion

There is merit in recruiting people who already share group identity. They could have a common working background, or may have faced redundancy problems together or they may live in the same village community. Others may be assimilated into the group through a network of friends and relatives and some firms successfully use this method as their main basis of recruitment. Where there is some form of social support, the middle-aged seem less inclined to cling for their security to their status. They are more ready to laugh at the problems and resign themselves to the junior role which training inevitably brings.

Respecting adult status

If training involves some loss of status, care can be taken to ensure that the adult trainee's sense of personal dignity is maintained. The instructor's superiority in social position rests only on his greater skill in the subject to be taught and it would be better for him to present himself as a colleague. If he belongs to the same age group his similarity in status will already be implied. There may be more problems with an instructor who is much older than his trainees. By contrast, an instructor who is younger than his trainees tends to show more deference to his class and it is not uncommon to find him being singled out by older trainees for special praise. Mutual respect sets the tone of relationships within the training school.

Getting the best out of mixed age groups

Most older trainees know their shortcomings as learners. They may also lack the technical expertise of many of their experienced but younger colleagues and fear that they may be 'shown up'. Yet the inclusion of young people in the training group is often associated with favourable results.* The training officer has a chance of getting the most out of a mixed group by building on the confidence and enthusiasm of the younger trainees and the maturity and conceptual searching of the older members. Where older trainees find that they are making some recognized contribution to the training group—for example by asking vital questions that draw out important answers—they become increasingly conscious of their special role and responsibilities in the group.

Matching the instructor to the trainees

The relationship between the trainee and his instructor is the

* *See* Research note by ITRU, 'Should older recruits be trained separately?' *Industrial and Commercial Training*, **1**, No. 2, 63, 1969.

most crucial of all the relationships. It may seem to defy analysis as to why one relationship should succeed and another fail, but one useful remedy for flagging progress in a trainee is to change his instructor. Some temperamental affinity, some changes in approach may spark off a new attitude.

It is often useful to search for the instructor who has a good approach to adult trainees. The most acceptable is sometimes one who has himself learned during adulthood and who is near in age and spirit to those he is teaching.

Consolidating after training

Older learners tend to stay longer in employment than youngsters once they overcome the main difficulties which reside in training and in transfer to the shop floor. Some of these shop floor difficulties reflect the failure of supervision to realize that the transferee from training will not be fully integrated into the system for some time, especially if he is middle-aged. The problems are more likely to be social and psychological in origin rather than a consequence of poor learning.

If sound personal relationships have been built up during training, the training officer and the instructor must keep closely in touch with their trainee. During that critical period when he is first adjusting to the job, there will always be some feature that differs from its training counterpart. Help from someone the trainee knows and trusts will relieve the aggravations. More important still is the role of such a person as a temporary communicator with the supervisor until the trainee has established his own social network.

6. Self-improvement

INTRODUCTION: THE USE OF THE TRAINEE'S INITIATIVE

Education and training taken together involve two sets of people. On the one hand are the organizers, teachers, and instructors, full of skill, status, and authority, which often they are only too anxious to display. On the other are the trainees who stand like initiates awaiting the ceremonies to be performed on their behalf. The in-group/out-group image is a real obstacle to the attraction of adults into training, but it seems to disappear wherever training can be conceived as an extension of work and the trainee feels he is 'on the inside' from the beginning or where the experience has partly come about at his own bidding.

Adults sometimes take a hand in organizing their own learning and when they do so their involvement is deep; self-consciousness disappears, and the results are generally commendable. Unfortunately, training and self-government are barely reconcilable. How can we train people to perform and yet leave them to themselves? One solution to this dilemma has been by developing principles and practices embodied under the 'discovery' method of training, which we have described more fully elsewhere.* Certainly some of the experiences described in this chapter contributed to the formation of our ideas on these principles.

*See (1) Belbin, R. M. *The Discovery Method: An International Experiment in Retraining.* In the series Employment of Older Workers. Paris: OECD, 1969 (available from HMSO); and (2) Belbin, R. M. *The Discovery Method of Training.* Training Information Paper No. 5. London: HMSO, 1969.

All the case studies in this chapter deal with systems that allow adults to play some part in organizing their own learning and in so doing they are giving recognition to a basic and perhaps primitive need. An adult is not a dependent, and provision for his training must be made on non-dependency lines.

The cases start with one that owes nothing to the plans of institutions, firms or instructors and we are allowed a rare glimpse of the conditions that emerge when adults set out to fulfil their own learning needs. The Mutual Improvement Classes have a long and as yet unrecorded history stretching back into the earliest days of the railways, when a skilled position was keenly sought after. So self-evident was it that unskilled workers would wish to assimilate the skills of the higher grades and by so doing put themselves in line for promotion that the management felt no economic motive or moral obligation to involve itself in training. Learning was a social process and one which developed such a tradition that it has survived to the present day.

The Mutual Improvement Class appears as an anachronism in an age when training demands great technical expertise. But home study is no anachronism. A relatively recent development of the correspondence course, it has proved an effective way of linking self-organization in learning with the technology of modern training. In the U.S.A., for example, sections of the steel industry have reaped substantial benefits from a training strategy very similar to that of the home study course outlined here. Workers study at home in their spare time and receive periodic tuition from instructors at practical working sessions. A singular feature, however, is that they are lent teaching machines to take home and they interchange the programmes in cassettes at regular intervals. Another development in Britain is, of course, the Open University linking television programmes with private tutorials.

This chapter suggests some of the advantages which home study offers for self-organization. Home study not only appears as an effective means of learning, but it appeals to groups who may be unable or reluctant to take advantage of other types of training facility.

The third case study describes a form of training that seems more akin to the relationship between the 'Oxbridge' under-graduate and his tutor than to an operator and his instructor in industry. It shows something of the way in which the trainee develops through the cultivation of the feeling that he is training himself, and of the particular advantage which the whole process offers for the firm.

The next topic touches on self-assessment as the principle upon which self-organization in training can revolve. The study comes from the Centre Universitaire de Co-opération Economique et Sociale (C.U.C.E.S.) at Nancy, France. Under the direction of M. Schwartz, this establishment has played an important part in raising the standard of basic education amongst mature adults who are held back educationally from undertaking advanced courses of vocational training. The educational deficiencies of adults excite a high degree of embarrassment which itself can be the main barrier to advancement. The older adult is frightened of being shown up before the group, before his teacher, even perhaps before himself. How can he reconcile his need to improve himself with his desire to protect his image? C.U.C.E.S. found one way by giving him precise feedback of his own progress, and by providing knowledge of group progress to the teachers without making public any information about the scores or shortcomings of individuals: not even the teacher knows the individual details. So if the adult learner needs to rectify his own deficiencies and the general programme fails to cover this adequately, he has to take the initiative in tutorials with his teacher. The idea is that through learning to assess him-self he also learns to organize himself.

The final study suggests one way in which an organization can develop retraining to meet the social as well as the skill challenge when a break in technology demands the refashion-ing of jobs. There is no ready-made blueprint of operations to be imposed on the men who will operate a mechanical cargo handling plant at Dublin Airport, for uncertainties must remain until the equipment has arrived and been installed. Yet this weakness is turned into a boon as training takes a surprising turn. The cargo handlers learn to identify the problems and the likely solutions for themselves while they practise some of the known elements of the new skills in simulated exercises. The reluctance of the training department to lay down precise rules in the first instance, while received initially with shock and disbelief, stimulates the men into active collaboration, for as they improve themselves they deepen their sense of personal responsibility.

Common to these case studies is a glimpse of how the adult trainee responds when the training situation offers an extra measure of latitude for trainee initiative.

1. MUTUAL-IMPROVEMENT: THE FORERUNNER OF FORMAL TRAINING

Mutual Improvement Classes (M.I.C.) began about a century ago as an expression of the appetite for self-improvement among artisans, particularly those employed in the operation of the new steam-driven machinery on the railways. No formal provision existed for the training of these men, who therefore set up their own groups or classes where, essentially, the better informed imparted their empirically won 'know-how' to the less experienced. In some sections of British Rail they have defied extinction by the competitive threat of modern training. Has their dynamism a message for the present day?

As the history of the M.I.C. movement on the railways of Great Britain has yet to be written, information about its early days is scarce. Classes seem to have been formed independently at the engine-sheds and to have flourished and then declined, only to be revived as enthusiasm re-awakened or some personality breathed new life into a dying class.

The railway companies provided no apprenticeship nor instruction for foot-plate staff whose sole ambition was to become engine drivers. The older companies did little even to assist or encourage the M.I.C. movement. They gave somewhat grudging provision of a room, limited permission to demonstrate on an engine in the shed, and little more. Often this came from the benevolence of the local fireman or shedmaster rather than from the formal assent of higher management. Yet, when the promotion system for foot-plate staff was firmly settled, the Mutual Improvement Class became the agency whereby the engine-cleaner prepared himself to 'pass the inspector' for promotion to the rank of fireman, and the fireman for promotion to driver.

The way to their goal was long and arduous for it depended entirely on their own initiative. Mr. Sam Sutcliffe, for example, was a cleaner for 21 years before he became a fireman, and was aged 46 when he was made driver. During the period of his career, economic depression brought normal promotion almost to a stop, but at all times it was a slow process.

When British Railways were nationalized in 1948, the obligation to train staff was written into the Act, and the new Railway Executive then took formal notice of the existence of the M.I.C. and prepared to lend assistance. The reaction of the movement was interesting: it asserted its independence and avoided the acceptance of any help which it thought might lead to the intervention of management in its affairs. Two positive results were apparent, however. Management, since 1950, has afforded systematic training for M.I.C. instructors, as part of the railway's training programme. It has also instituted a 'quiz' competition, in which teams trained by M.I.C. from all over the system compete in answering intricate questions on locomotive management and the application of running rules.

The movement is now in decline. This is perhaps inevitable. The social and industrial conditions which prompted its originators to start it, and their successors to keep it alive, have in the main departed. Engine-men do not, perhaps, regard their calling as a vocation to the same degree as their predecessors. The steam locomotive was a relatively simple device, whereas a diesel or electric locomotive is a complex machine, and training in its use and management is a matter for skilled instruction. The duty of providing it is now fully accepted by British Rail.

Mr. Sutcliffe doubts, however, whether the driver of the future will respond without the incentive which enthused his predecessors. He doubts whether a man posted to a training course will have the same interest as the man who, of his own volition, attended his M.I.C. to learn his job and earn his promotion. He recounted for ITRU the fortunes and the character of the York M.I.C. over the past forty-odd years in a conversation with Mr. J. Kirkby Thomas.

SS: When I came to York in 1916, I was 13, and I went to join a school. The school would not admit me, so I went to work as an errand boy in a grocer's shop. The wage for the week was ten shillings. I continued to work there and in two years the war ended. Then I asked for a rise and got the sack. I was out of work for a year or so and in the end I joined the railway company, in 1920, as an engine cleaner. From there I progressed over the years (sometimes very slow years) from engine cleaner to fireman—actually it was twenty-one years before I got the name 'fireman'. This was in the worst years of the depression. I progressed to driver in 1949, for after World War II we were promptly made drivers and given mates immediately. We should have been made 'Driver' before but couldn't be promoted until there were firemen to go with us.

In 1951 I was appointed as a temporary firing instructor, getting the permanent appointment in 1959, and when dieselization came, I achieved my ambition and became diesel instructor at the Diesel Training School at York.

I joined the M.I.C. straightaway in 1920. It's a long time ago to look back on. How did I come to join?

Well, I think in those days the old men were rather eager to get the youngsters in, and the first thing they asked you to do was to join the Union, and at the Union you were asked to join the M.I.C. In those days it didn't mean too much to me, but following along with all the rest, I joined. I paid sixpence. That was the fee to become a member of M.I.C.

JKT: Where did you meet?

SS: We met at what was then the Railway Institute in York. We had one room there; very small, shared by three classes. There was the clerical side; there was the ambulance; we had the M.I.C. side. All we were provided with was the room. As three different sets of people occupied it, it was totally impossible to have diagrams, models or anything. And everything we wanted had to be brought out of boxes, used and tidily put away.

JKT: You met on Sunday mornings?

SS: Every Sunday morning from half-past ten to noon. I can see now one of the leaders who used to do it. He had a long beard and was very much respected. He was a driver, and a driver of the real old school. All he ever spoke about was on one subject and one subject only—and I still know a lot about it—the Westinghouse brake. To us young cleaners, the Westinghouse brake seemed a terrible thing. There was no blackboard to put any illustration on; there were no maps, there were no diagrams; there was nothing— just our friend with the long beard, telling us all about it, and it was difficult to get it over.

About five men ran the class; one would take the engine, one would take the brake, one would take the rules (in those days the least thought about), and so on. I think we had about four protection rules; no others were ever discussed. The lack of facilities held us back very much. We learned something but not a tremendous deal. We had *one* model which is still in the possession of the York M.I.C. This was made at the Old Queen Street Locomotive Works in 1898. It was a model of Stephenson's gear. It was handmade, and we still have the bill for it.

JKT: Did you have to order it from the works and pay for it through the class?

SS: This model was paid for out of contributions. We hadn't much money in those days. After we had paid our initial sixpence to become a member, we were supposed to give at least twopence each Sunday we attended. Not everyone gave twopence; sometimes you said you would give it the next Sunday, because you hadn't got it. But these twopences mounted up and they always went to educational purposes—to get diagrams. Sometimes we did borrow items from the shed but these were usually promptly reclaimed. Instruction went on in this way for about five years, to the best of my recollection, and then we moved. The classes were always moving in those days. It seemed that we settled in a room and then on some excuse we had to be moved on. At one time we went into the doctor's room. We stayed there about nine months; no more. Nobody wanted us. So once more we moved on; this time into a 'classroom', and this was the messroom. Messrooms aren't the best places, even at 10.30 on a Sunday morning. It was totally impossible for anyone to go into a messroom on a Sunday morning with a reasonable suit on. So it was just like being at work— you put your overalls on. It wasn't a room where you could speak freely—we always had interlopers in telling us where we were wrong. That lasted quite a while. Then we were fortunate to be given an old room—it took weeks to make it habitable. But we washed it and we dusted it; and this was the beginning of the M.I.C. in York, as we know it today. We were at last able to display models in this room, and anything that we could get hold of; that was the beginning of the present collection of models and diagrams that we got over the years.

JKT: You still had drivers as instructors?

SS: The usual thing was that you had drivers as instructors. And I want to be quite candid with you. Many times over the years in the Mutual Improvement Class, we were glad of anyone who would instruct us. Personally, I was first a pupil in the M.I.C. but I was also an instructor while still a cleaner. I hadn't the name 'fireman' and I was a long time in getting it—but after about five years as cleaner I would stand up and have a go myself instructing the class. Occasionally there were drivers present, usually very few in number—because we found that as soon as a fireman had achieved his object and been made an engine-driver, he wasn't often seen again.

JKT: Did you ever have any old-timers who would come along, week by week, for the interest of it?

SS: Yes. I remember one man in particular. His name was Bill Dunn and he was an old-timer when he came to York. He was a wonderful old man; he got struck down by multiple sclerosis, but he attended to the end. We would pay for him to come on a Sunday morning and he would come and go home by taxi.

JKT: Can you tell me something about the organization of your M.I.C.? You had a chairman and secretary, didn't you?

SS: Oh yes, and we had a set of rules—a very stringent set of rules. These were formed much earlier in the existence of the class—long before I remember it, because the class was formed before the 1900s. These rules were made in 1893 when the York Mutual Improvement Class was founded.

Rule One. The Mutual Improvement Class was meant for cleaners, firemen and drivers, and no-one outside was ever allowed to come into the class. So it remains to this day. People could be admitted as guests

but in the normal way you had to be a cleaner, a fireman or a driver. When I reached supervisory rank in
1962, after forty-odd years in the class, I got a vote
of thanks and that was the end of my career in
the Mutual Improvement Class. They had a chairman—they had a secretary—they had a committee
which would vary from time to time. These would
all have been elected by those of the members
present.

JKT: Can we go back to the organization? You kept minutes?

SS: Oh yes, we kept minutes. The minute book, especially
the original one, is very interesting to look at because
they kept their minute books religiously in those days;
far better than we did. The original one in York you
can see at any time. It's well bound in vellum binding;
it's in copper-plate writing and is really interesting.
They recorded everything: how many were there, just
what was done, and so on.

JKT: Yes. I noticed that occasionally you could have an
engine in steam in the shed.

SS: Yes, but that came later. It says in the records: 'a
request was made to Mr. Brown, the night-shed foreman, to have a locomotive in steam' so they could take
the big end down. Very practical. They would provide
anything practical, as long as when we took it down, we
put it back, or the fitting was quite all right when we
returned it. And it was costing them nothing, except
for the man who helped, say, to take the piston down
or centralize the valve.

JKT: Was there any connection with other M.I.C.s?

SS: Not in the early days, but in the early thirties there
was a move to get a Federation of Mutual Improvement Classes, and this came about. We joined at York
and became a member of the Federated Mutual Improvement Society. We met other societies, but only
on odd occasions. I think in the end I am right in
saying that, in the forties, meetings died away—to be

revived with the coming of the quiz competition of the Federation.

JKT: When did the class really settle down to the task—a very narrow task, I imagine—of training people to pass the inspector?

SS: When we got a room of our own. From then onwards, a great search was made for models and diagrams, and I think in my own way that this was the start of our Mutual Improvement Class as we knew it over the last twenty or thirty years, because then we were able to display anything we got. We borrowed, we begged, we—well we won't call it stealing—borrowed anything for as long as the foreman didn't borrow it back again. We had a blackboard. We also made a little railway. And we paid for it ourselves. An 'O' gauge railway, signals and everything: sidings and points and so on.

JKT: How far did the men play a part in discussion in a lecture?

SS: A few of them did say something and that would probably get discussions going; just a word here or a question there, starting a little discussion; and how large it might grow! They could do us quite a lot of good by starting the ball rolling. Of course, we always had the man who came just to be awkward. We generally got rid of him.

JKT: Was there any move to discourage anyone who wasn't a good instructor?

SS: Well, over the years we had many who were good men who would make a request. They would say, 'I would like to teach'. Many tried, but I am afraid very few really made it. They had the knowledge. They had everything that it takes except the one thing—they couldn't put it across. And this happened so many times. It was quite a pity. A man with the necessary knowledge could be dumb when it came to standing in front of a blackboard with a piece of chalk in his hand. So if he couldn't do it we had quite politely to suggest to him that it was no use.

JKT: Would you like to tell me something about the social aspect of the M.I.C. movement?

SS: There was one point that I always feel sorry about. That was the rule that excluded the wives of the members. We ourselves went on many outings, but never in all that time in the Mutual Improvement Class did we have a day when our wives could take their place. I always thought this was wrong—very wrong. There were hours and hours when I could have been with my wife but I was at the Mutual Improvement Class. I ran a class of my own on Monday night for years and spent hours away from my wife, but we were never to get over this social ban on having mixed company. I think it was a survival from the old days when the old men said 'No! The wife's place is at home', so she had to stop at home.

JKT: Did you ever go over a locomotive works—say at Darlington?

SS: To Darlington? Once, but Doncaster was our favourite place. Personally, I have been to Crewe, and Ashford in Kent, too.

JKT: What was the reaction of the class when a new type of locomotive came in?

SS: I think the revolutionary part on the old North-Eastern was when after we had been used all the years to Stephenson valve gear, we received locomotives with the Walschaerts gear. This was something tremendous and we had to realize that this was something we had really to get to grips with. We had to master this Walschaerts gear, followed by the Gresley-Walschaerts, which proved to be a complicated gear which once again gave us the incentive to get down to it. It wasn't so much the locomotive itself, but when you got a revolutionary change of gear of that description then the Mutual Improvement Class was pretty busy.

JKT: I suppose people came in great numbers, and the classes grew until they had got it mastered. Then what?

SS: In the long run, looking back honestly over the years, the thing that really made the Mutual Improvement Class tick was when there was the chance that someone was going to 'pass the Inspector'. During my career, one particular period of seven years went by and no one went on to become a driver. There was no need for more drivers. The class got smaller and smaller until, in the end, there were only a faithful few. Perhaps five of us in number. Sometimes only one would come to a lesson on a Sunday morning. Many were wanting to cease activities, to disband the class, but I always said 'No! We owe something to the men of the 1890s and 1900s. No, we won't leave go whatever happens'. And it has been the same all my career. We've kept it going.

JKT: Could you, Sam, give us your reflections on the future of the movement? Do you think it is going to survive or do you think it will die out?

SS: This is so difficult: we live in such tremendously changing times. We can only guess, however much we should like to know. I have severed my connection with the M.I.C., but I know that I quite sincerely would never like to see the movement die. I don't think it can die. If it does die, what are we going to get in its place? We can't let it die. But still, on the other hand, how can we make it survive? Who is going to do it? In what face, shape or form could it keep its place?

JKT: The railway now does accept the duty of training. Can *they* not put something in its place?

SS: The place of the movement shrinks as British Rail takes over the duties of training the men, with the facilities and resources they can offer. But to me the thing that seems lacking is that M.I.C.s were attended by those who were interested; and there is the point—

interested. If you get a man and you say he must go for tuition, it's a different thing altogether from the man who said all those years ago: 'I am going because I love my work and am interested in my work'. The same as the men who taught: they had no thought of any gain. They taught simply because they wanted to teach, because they liked teaching. And those that came liked to learn. And I am afraid for the future. I hope I am wrong but I think we shall lose that something that we have had for a hundred years'.

Adequate premises, equipment, finance, and instructional expertise eluded the M.I.C. during most of its history. Nevertheless, in a closely-knit world (from whose social activities women were excluded) teaching and learning were natural processes that gave coherence to the group. The needs of learners were met by those who felt capable of satisfying them. Remarkable feats of human energy and inventive enterprise secured the only working models they obtained. The men trained each other, yet never used the word training. They were engaging in 'mutual improvement', an activity which combined the notions of personal development with the sense of responsibility to fellows and workmates.

The hard-ware of training is now liberally endowed in many companies and often takes highly sophisticated forms. But is that 'something', which Sam Sutcliffe fears is missing, the 'spirit of mutuality' which permeated human relationships within the M.I.C.?

2. QUALIFYING AS A BOILER OPERATOR BY HOME STUDY

Most of the case histories in this book have been concerned with the training of men and women within an industrial organization. But what happens when a man sees his way clear to promotion yet is left to organize his own training? One possibility for self-improvement is to use the facilities of a local technical college. In fact those who avail themselves of these facilities in middle age have been shown in surveys to consist mainly of 'regulars' in adult education or persons already holding considerable expertise in the subject matter of the course. The chances are that the man who is most in need of technical education is unlikely to break into the technical college environment on his own, especially when the factors that make for success (father-figure instructors, group membership and so on) are all absent from the picture. Lastly there is the physical barrier. The type of highly specialized course that he considers relevant to his needs may not be available nor lie within easy travelling distance. This is where the alternative of the correspondence or home study course comes into its own and the boiler operator is a good example of the man for whom such a course is ideally designed.

Problems of a boiler-man

Boiler operators are found in small groups in many different industries—for example, in electricity generating and mining. They are also employed in the heating plants of public baths, hospitals and factories where oil or solid fuel is used to generate steam pressure for process work or for central heating. Thus although collectively they form a large group, there are not always a sufficient number employed in one place or available for release simultaneously to justify internal training schemes.

The home study course designed for boilermen involves the equivalent of seventy hours of technical college instruction in preparation for the City & Guilds of London Institute's Boiler Operator's Certificate. How does the older worker get on if he can be lured as far as registering for this course? What kind of people take home study courses, and why? Do they pass their examinations? What are their problems? Who are the most successful? Do they like the courses?

These were the main questions when, at the suggestion of the National Coal Board, ITRU investigated the usefulness of the home study courses which the N.C.B. had pioneered in 1959 for its operatives in conjunction with the College of Fuel Technology.

The course and the examination

Three large organizations were offering home study courses for the City and Guilds examination: N.C.B., Central Electricity Generating Board, and National Industrial Fuel Efficiency Service. A common feature of these courses is that a weekly quota of theory is studied, and the answers to questions are sent to a tutor who returns them with marks and comments. In itself, this would be no different from a conventional correspondence course; however, the additional advantage of this particular form of home study is that students attend periodic meetings with an instructor who teaches them the practical side of the work, and who can resolve difficulties in the theory which individuals have not been able to solve. Work for the practical part of the examination is being done all the time on the job. The men are shown both laboratory demonstrations and films, and visits are arranged where possible to different plants. This means that trainees can work on the theory at their own pace, re-reading sections which are difficult and looking back at anything which has been forgotten, while at work and at group meetings they can relate theory to practice.

The examination is in two parts: theory and practical. The theory paper consists of some essay type questions together with a series of other short questions requiring the minimum of writing (this allows for candidates who find writing a slow or difficult process). The practical test is conducted on a plant with which the candidate is familiar, preferably the one at which he normally works.

Having learned about the course, our next step was to find out who took it and to what effect. It transpired that 305 U.K. candidates had completed the course for that year, 244 through a home study course, thirty-three through technical colleges and twenty-eight as a result of 'in-plant' training. Forty-nine of those finishing the course were over the age of 50, a good proportion by the normal standards in adult education.

Follow-up questionnaires were sent to all candidates and 178 were returned. Analysis of these showed that home study course takers, in contrast with those taking other courses, were more likely to be volunteers than 'referrals' by the company and that the volunteer rate was higher for the over-40s than for the under-40s. In other words, home study courses had a special appeal to the older learner and this was further shown by the response of all candidates, irrespective of course when given a choice between following a home study and a technical college course.

Some of the difficulties mentioned on college courses helped to underline the usefulness of home study. These difficulties centred on travel and fitting in with shift work. Some of the men worked in such small units that it would be extremely difficult to fill the gap if anyone missed a shift to go to evening classes.

Other difficulties cited by the formal class students included 'writing, spelling, and taking notes'. In this aspect, the home study groups were probably at an advantage. For them note-taking is only of marginal importance as the students work from well-prepared and documented material. Those at technical colleges, on the other hand, are obliged to depend on notes for they are less likely to be presented with a comprehensive set of hand-outs by their teacher. In fact, note-taking is a skill, one that complements the lecturer's mode of presentation, but it is a skill seldom well developed amongst adults who left school at an early age.

The older home study men described 'concentration' as one of their main worries but this did not seem due to the physical distractions of family life. Here it was the younger home study men who suffered most—'... I have children aged 2 and 3 years and I find it almost impossible to isolate myself for any length of time to get into my books'. The older man has less occasion for being interrupted in his studies: his children will have grown up or be at the homework stage themselves.

The difficulty in concentrating may be due to a lack of stimulation and here the lecturer has a distinct advantage in being able to hold attention and focus thought. But, if the older men were sufficiently absorbed by their material, the conditions of home study provided a setting which assisted their learning in many ways. The most favourable aspects were 'being able to study in complete privacy' and 'working at your own pace'. 'Home study gives one more time to concentrate', '... this way the older man who does not normally catch on as quickly as the younger man ... can pick things up in his own time'. And as one man of 60 commented, '... home study seems more suited to my age ... other forms of training seem more high-pressure'. A 47-year-old trainee said, 'the older man on the first day appears to lose some of his confidence; he thinks he will never sort it out. He does, of course, but that first impression is important'. This loss of confidence may well be greater if the 'older man' has to cope with strange surroundings as well as strange subjects.

The main impression from talking to five older men in their individual homes two years after the course was of their great enthusiasm for home study. Mr. King, a 51-year-old, had only one reservation. He would have liked more practical application. Although he was working with boilers every day, he felt the need for an instructor who could have supervised this work to tell him if and where he was going wrong.

They all had high praise for the instructors and organization of the course. Four of them thought it had been well worth while and, faced with making the same decision again, they would have no hesitation in undergoing the training.

If there had been any difficulties in adjusting to studying at home, they certainly didn't remember them two years later. They didn't think the courses had resulted in any particular disturbance to their home or social life (the youngest man interviewed was 39). Perhaps this is not altogether surprising since one informant volunteered the news that some of them did their 'home' study in the quiet hours of the evening shift!

What was the outcome?

Did they pass the exams? It seemed that not only were large numbers of older people willing to take home study courses, but from the overall marks those who did so were very successful. Of those over the age of 40, 80·8 per cent passed the home study course, a figure almost comparable to the 81·4 per cent for younger men.

A further measure of success arising out of the popularity of home study must be that many were introduced to the idea of retraining from amongst those who would have been reluctant or unable to attend more formal classes—and the introduction paid dividends, at least on examination results.

Some other benefits

Promotion. Of the five people interviewed only one considered that his added qualifications had been of direct benefit as far as job status was concerned and even for him promotion was still a thing of the future.

Added knowledge. The trainees visited were far from being disgruntled at taking a course which did not lead to promotion. They thought that they had gained breadth of interest, a great deal more knowledge and an appreciation of the intricacies of the job. One was sure he had increased in skill and claimed among other advantages that he had cut down his domestic fuel bills—he now applied his new knowledge to lighting his fires at home!

Many of the questionnaire replies indicated that having carried out the job for several years with no theoretical knowledge, they were now delighted with the fact that they knew 'how' and 'why'.

One man said that since going on the course he felt more secure. He had special problems in learning. He was deaf. Others too said that completing the course had increased their self-confidence and made them feel more sure of their ability to do the job well.

Further learning?

From many of the replies in the questionnaires (and often from long letters voluntarily attached to them) it was clear that the men had got something more than direct benefits from the course. One man of 56 commented, 'If I pass or fail it hasn't been a waste of time'. Another said, '...I wish it went on indefinitely'. In many cases it seemed that the men had gained real satisfaction in finding that they were capable of concentrated study. One interviewee claimed he hadn't gone on any further since taking the course, but admitted that he had been sending for library books on boiler efficiency to 'learn a bit more'. One wonders how much the introduction to this form of study might have stimulated the older participants generally towards further study. Would they be willing to go on to technical college courses on another occasion? The five men interviewed by ITRU were very hesitant about this. '...if we were taught in a way suitable for older people'; '...if I knew just what was involved'; '...not if it involved a lot of maths or memory work'. In fact, all their comments were prefaced with 'if'.

The reader may ask why we concern ourselves with the question of inducement to further learning. Surely the 'home studiers' had achieved their objective? Our interest in continuity of learning was aroused by scrutiny of the previous experience of the boiler operators and of other examinees studying for a closely related City & Guilds examination—Coal Preparation Certificate. Of eighty-nine candidates for the latter examination, forty-five had continued some form of education since leaving school and before taking the training course; forty-four had not. An interesting and distinctive pattern emerged on the theory examination for candidates who in other respects—e.g. their job history and practical test marks—would seem equal. Those who had continued education gained on average much higher marks than those who had not. For example, the mean score of the continuers in their 40s was 69·4 and for those in their 50s it was 62·3. The comparable figures for the non-continuers were 53·1 and 48·5.

It could not be the *content* of the 'further education' which assisted the passing of the theory examinations. In very few cases was it relevant. Art, commerce, first aid, history, music, public speaking, wireless telegraphy, trade union law—these were typical of the subjects studied. It seems that continued learning, itself, towards which home study may make a significant contribution, can keep alive learning skills and indicate those likely to make the best prospects on training courses.

The success of this experiment seemed to point to some intrinsic merits in home study for older, unskilled and under-educated workers. Home study offers privacy and a chance for the unpracticed learner to grapple with the problems slowly, at his own pace, allowing him plenty of opportunity to develop his own imagery. Can it be that this approach offers one of the rare entry points into further education for a section of the population usually conspicuous for non-attendance? And are we ready to develop this path further?

3. SELF-TRAINING THROUGH A FACTORY PROJECT

Almost every company has problems in the redeployment of its personnel. These arise from time to time when a whole section faces shut-down but also as everyday events, such as a medical recommendation for lighter work or the reorganization of job, materials or lay-out which reduce the staff required by one or two. For a multitude of policy reasons, a company will try to find an alternative job, even if it is a job for which the individual is not ideally suited.

In this connection, Procter and Gamble Ltd., the detergent manufacturers of Newcastle-upon-Tyne, have carried their obligation as employer one step further by offering a contract

or guarantee of regular employment which comes into operation two years after an employee has joined the company. In
effect, an employee is offered the eventual security of a
minimum annual wage. The guarantee refers however to
employment and not to a man's specific job. The security
which protects a man from dismissal save for misconduct is
made possible by a training policy which ensures that workers
are equipped to switch from one job to another as the need
arises. This can result in some loss of take-home pay for the
worker due to variations in bonus earnings, but it is a small
price to pay for employment security. Evidently the policy is
highly acceptable to workers in practice, if labour turnover is
any guide. This dropped from 46 per cent for all factory
employees to 18 per cent, the latter at a time when the national
average for manufacturing industry was 31.5 per cent.
Amongst 'guaranteed' employees in the company it has fallen
to 6.5 per cent.

Mr. A, aged 55, had been employed by Procter and Gamble
on production work for twenty years when, following a heart
attack, he was referred for other work. As often happens, the
alternative jobs available were at a relatively high level of
skill and one post vacant was that of factory materials inspector. This job demanded a good deal of independence and
initiative in coping with various materials and stock problems throughout the entire factory. The responsibilities
seemed to extend a good deal beyond those to which Mr. A
had been accustomed during his work in production although
he had risen to the level of charge-hand.

It was a typical policy decision of Procter and Gamble that
Mr. A should be trained for this new job, although most
other organizations would have considered it outside his
reach. The fact that such a decision could be implemented
with some measure of confidence is testimony to the discern-
ing way in which training is organized. The primary responsibility for training rests on the departmental manager who
draws up a training programme to suit the needs of each
individual. The departmental manager is assisted by the

factory training specialist who can interpret the objectives of the exercise in terms of knowledge about training.

The main feature of the programme is project work, a form of training more commonly employed for newly recruited graduates, who respond favourably to it because they see it as a challenge. For those less well educated it has other advantages. Learning through a project or task largely offsets the need to conduct training through words either in spoken (lecture) form or in writing. Moreover, it affords a continuous stream of information to the instructor—in this case the receiving manager—about how the trainee is faring and what features of the work are presenting difficulties.

Project work documentation

While the primary need is to develop direct experience, the programme does start with a certain amount of written documentation, defining and describing the job, laying down the standards of performance expected and naming the person to whom the job-holder is answerable.

Mr. A was not at all conversant with paper work and for him the descriptions were concise and to the point—'You will be expected to conduct accurate stock-taking of packing materials, raw materials, and process materials' ... 'You will be expected to convey accurate information about stock' ... 'You will be expected to conduct other checks as assigned to you by your manager' ...

The programme then explained the documents which he should understand, consult, and study. He was advised about accounts and orders which were available for study.

He was next given his specific training assignments:

1. For each department in the factory he was, for example, to
   (*a*) list all points where material wastage could occur; note whether the scrap could be reprocessed and whether it should feature in the month-end inventory;
   (*b*) write down all materials used by the department and where the materials were stored.

2. Write down all sampling methods used.
3. Read department inventory systems documents. Note any that were out of date and inaccurate and list any improvements necessary.
4. Carry out the following inventories:
   (some half dozen inventories from different departments were specified).

The list continued through a further four training assignments.

Under the heading of 'Safety', the programme stated that the objective was to enable the materials inspector to recognize the extent of his responsibility. He was advised to read and study certain background information. He was to acquaint himself with the safety rules of the receiving department, along with those of the other departments. He was to survey the materials handling and stacking methods in the factory, and list any safety items which he considered worthy of discussion with the safety manager. Finally he was told that his safety test would be supervised by both the department manager and the safety manager.

Trainee solves his own problems

Mr. A required a good deal of clarification, explanation and prompting from his departmental manager before he was able to start. But in due course he was able to establish his own priorities in the programme and decide how to allot his time to respective items. He went on to develop his own job control book which has since proved a valuable reference. This was no small achievement for a man of 55 who had spent most of his life as a production operative.

Mr. A's main problems which became apparent at the intermediate stage test were his tendency to be unduly dominated by consideration of production and by a failure to reorient his thinking towards a factory-wide assignment. These tendencies, however, were discussed from time to time with his manager and eventually overcome. Mr. A went on to gain both intermediate and final qualifications. He subsequently undertook and developed his new responsibilities in a very satisfactory manner. His comments on the method were that the programme itself had given a very clear guide and that the stage tests had provided a strong incentive.

The project method of training, being individually tailored, has no set time allowance for completion although there are expectations on how long each programme will last. Progress in training at Procter and Gamble depends on how well an individual organizes himself, which he can do in one of two ways: to complete the tasks assigned to him with expediency and to a satisfactory standard (the effect of which is to complete the training within the target training time); or to pursue the tasks in some depth (with the attendant possibility that the target time will be overrun). This somewhat open situation brings out the characteristic differences between individuals.

For example, Mr. B, aged 35, and Mr. C, aged 24, appeared to the training manager to be men of similar calibre. Both were employed on grade 3 jobs, one a labourer and the other a cleaner. Both had been referred for training as grade 1 process operators to control a chemical reactor, involving the taking of acidity tests and the control of temperature. The process worker is expected to carry out a number of routine tasks with care and precision, but faults sometimes occur and it is the measure of the most able process worker that he can recognize them at an early stage and take appropriate action.

Both workers were given the same training assignments (although they started at different times). Mr. C, enjoying the characteristics of the younger man, required only half the time of Mr. B to complete his project assignments and ran into no obvious difficulties during the training. But while quick to learn, his knowledge was regarded as superficial. Later he was referred for a further period of training when it became apparent that he lacked some of the 'extra' qualities of the good process operator.

Mr. B, by contrast, ran into difficulties with two of his

assignments. The shortcomings were discussed with his manager who was able to help him to complete the tasks. Mr. B gradually increased his confidence and his understanding of the new work in spite of the fact that his training had fallen behind schedule. His progress, however, continued. Some months after he had been transferred to process control work as a grade 1 operator, he was recognized as having an unusually good diagnostic approach to his job and was earmarked as a potential chargehand.

These three men have all fared differently under the project method of training. What stands out in the experience of the firm is the way in which the challenge to a trainee to organize himself in relation to his training objectives reveals the potentialities of the man.

4. SELF-ASSESSMENT AS A FOCAL POINT OF ADULT TRAINING

The Centre Universitaire de Co-opération Economique et Sociale (C.U.C.E.S.) at Nancy in France is well-known for its work in training full-time students to professional levels required in all sections of industry, commerce and local government. One of its departments (P.S.T.—Promotion Superieur du Travail) specializes in training adult men and women who are already in employment but who wish to qualify in their trade or profession, or to prepare themselves for promotion to more responsible levels.

The Director of the Centre, M. Bertrand Schwartz, has a long-standing interest in the development of methods for training men and women which enable them to adapt to the changes brought about by technological progress. If such training was successful, he has argued, it should help them to participate fully in the new society both at work and in leisure. But how could it be achieved, when traditional methods of teaching were so out of line with personal needs?

C.U.C.E.S. had been handling about 500 people each year, but this was a very small number compared with likely demands of the future, when the greater part of the working population would need occasional or even intermittent retraining at periods throughout working life.

Nor was it only a matter of scale. The classical procedures of instruction could not meet this new situation, for its orientation was towards the award of certificates and diplomas, rather than to a broadening in the outlook of the individual so that he could better adapt to vicissitudes of the modern world. This would place impossible pressures upon existing qualified teachers.

A further issue which concerned M. Schwartz was the different character of the new community of students. They were men and women from all types of social background, operating at many levels of knowledge, and employed in a wide range of organizations. The traditional method of instruction needed a modification of some sort if an optimum response was to be elicited from each student.

A different method of assessing the progress of students was the essential feature of M. Schwartz's modification. 'Self evaluation' was developed as a means of replacing the system of periodic tests and examinations corrected and marked by the instructor. His system was adopted as an integral part of the training process and it embraced both the trainee and the instructor.

Self-evaluation at C.U.C.E.S.

The evaluation system was applied from the time of enrolment and was effective throughout the year. 'As the training programme progresses', explained M. Schwartz, 'increasing importance is placed on the informative function of evaluation as the means by which the instructor regulates the training content and schedule. But first *we* start, as the organization responsible for training, by assessing the level of knowledge of the student at the time he enrols.'

The adult promotion course mainly comprises mathematics and the physical sciences, but it also includes training in industrial organization, communications, and general culture. There are four levels of entry known as 'years' A, B, C, and D. Each student is interviewed at the time of enrolment to give him information about the courses and in turn to collect from him details about his education and experience. During the interview, with the help of various tests, the student's existing knowledge is assessed in relation to the programmes of years A, B, C, and D so that he can be placed in the most appropriate level. Thus, some of the sources of discouragement and frustration are avoided and the student is introduced to the notion of self-evaluation—he can judge for himself where he stands at the outset *vis-à-vis* his fellow beginners. During the first term, this initial assessment is checked and if necessary the student may transfer to another year.

From the beginning, the syllabus is built around self-evaluation sessions which take place

(*a*) in the evening, four to five times per week;

(*b*) at the end of each term;

(*c*) at the end of the year.

Daily self-evaluation session

The evening study starts with a discourse given by the *professeur* lasting forty minutes, and finishes with 'group activity' lasting forty to forty-five minutes. The latter is controlled by an assistant, who stimulates among a group of ten or twelve students a discussion on the preceding lecture; or he might organize exercises for the group which involve the application of what has been taught to the sort of situations and problems likely to arise in their daily work.

In between these periods, twenty minutes are devoted to self-evaluation. At the end of his discourse, the *professeur* poses a problem or short questions designed to test understanding of the most important principle which he has tried to convey. Each student writes the answers to the questions on a sheet of paper bearing no mark of identification. At the finish of the exercise, the correct solutions are written on the blackboard. Students then correct their own work and they are asked to explain their errors at the foot of their paper. If their answers do not correspond with the solutions on the blackboard, they must decide whether they have:

(*a*) failed to understand the text of a question;
(*b*) made an error of calculation;
(*c*) misused a formula or used a wrong formula;
(*d*) forgotten something;
(*e*) made an error of reasoning, etc.;
(*f*) failed in some other way.

The papers are collected by the assistant, who makes out an analysis sheet which looks something like this:

Class   ....
Subject   ....
Questions ....

Number attending the class	50
Number of correct answers	35
Number of wrong answers	15
Number who misunderstood a principle	3
Number who made an error of calculation	8
Number who forgot a formula	2
Number who did not explain their error	2

After recording the group results the assistant checks each answer paper for the correct explanation of any error made. If a student has wrongly diagnosed the reason for an incorrect reply, or if he has omitted to explain his error, the assistant makes an appropriate note on the paper. The papers are returned to the classroom in a pile, so that students may take back their own when they arrive for the next class.

The analysis sheet is sent to the *professeur*, who can then judge his own effectiveness in the presentation of his material by taking account of the proportion of correct answers. The sheet will tell him whether or not he has achieved a reasonable measure of success with his class.

At the start of the next self-evaluation period, the analysis sheet is posted on the blackboard so that the individual student can identify himself among the 'correct answers' or the 'incorrect answers' and can see where he stands in relation to his class-mates.

M. Schwartz places great importance upon the fact that students correct and evaluate their own work. 'This practice acknowledges their adulthood and also has an informative function. By giving them sufficient information to evaluate their own work, they are coaxed into taking a mature and objective view of their results.'

The informative function depends upon the use students make of a personal record which they are encouraged to keep and which contains, in addition to the date and subject, their reply to questions (right or wrong); the reasons for errors; and the diagnosis of reason (right or wrong).

The completion of this record each day serves as a reminder of certain errors which may be recurring or of failure to diagnose the reason for mistakes, but it may also act as a measure of progress. The document remains in the personal possession of the student and is never seen by anyone else unless he chooses to show it to the *professeur* or his assistant, whilst seeking help or guidance.

End of term self-evaluation

The questions posed at the end of the term constitute an exercise which tests memory, comprehension and assimilation of the term's work. The results permit the student to see exactly how much he has gained and where he stands.

A meeting is held by the *professeur*, the psychologist, his assistants—who by now know very well each member of their group—and the student representatives of the whole class. Difficulties are discussed and the advice of the meeting is passed on to students at a private interview with the *professeur* or the psychologist.

End of year self-evaluation

Whilst it was normal practice for the Centre to advise a
student at the end of the year on his plans for the future, M.
Schwartz maintains that his students by that time are sufficiently accustomed to evaluating their progress and prospects
to be able to reach a decision themselves. At their disposal
they have:

(a) their own record of progress during the year;
(b) the outcome of interviews during the year with the *pro-
    fesseur* and the psychologist (convened either at the re-
    quest of the student or as a matter of course by the
    professeur or psychologist to discuss progress) and
(c) details about future openings.

The decision facing the student is a choice between four
courses of action:

(a) to repeat the course;
(b) to enrol at a higher level (i.e. year D, having completed
    year C or year B);
(c) to enrol for one year's full-time study for a state diploma
    (for which there are government grants equivalent to
    previous average earnings, and sometimes secondment
    by the employer);
(d) abandon further training of this sort and rely upon
    whatever promotion opportunities may present them-
    selves within his organization.

The preparation of the overall results of the year for presentation to the class forcibly involves the *professeur* in an
appraisal of the problems which have arisen during the year
and the remarks, suggestions, and criticisms made to him
during interviews. In the light of this study, his programme
can be reviewed, his method refashioned, and his techniques
improved.

Further extensions

The C.U.C.E.S. scheme began in 1964–65 when workers' representatives asked for a course which would enable miners in the Lorraine iron ore basin to receive more training. The first area for the experiment included twelve mines, and by the autumn of 1966, over 400 miners were being given training. Since 1967, the scheme has been extended to a second area, also with twelve mines, and is now open to all adults, miners or not. There are now 9,000 students, and in the first area, some have completed their fourth course. The subjects available have extended considerably from the original basic electricity, mathematics, mechanics, and drawing, and now range from dressmaking to business management.

In June 1966, students asked for facilities to qualify for a job proficiency certificate—C.A.P., Certificat d'Aptitude Professionnelle—and in 1967 a trial scheme was started using a course-credit system. With this method, the syllabus for an examination is divided into a number of training units and a credit is awarded for each successfully completed unit. Each student is thus able to build up to the total of needed credits at his own pace, in a way suited to his ability and knowledge already acquired, and to his available free time. C.A.P. is only awarded if all necessary credits have been obtained, and a system of common core credits makes it easier to acquire further C.A.P.s with a subsequent occupation change. Although this system has now superseded the programme of years A, B, C, and D described above, the principle of self-assessment and elimination of a final all-or-nothing examination remain integral features of the new development.

5. SELF INVOLVEMENT IN A NEW SYSTEM

When a highly mechanized handling and storage system was about to be set up at Dublin Airport to handle the ever-growing expansion of the cargo freight business, Cathal Mullen, then the staff training manager at Aer Lingus, and

Dr. Liam Gorman, of the Irish Management Institute, came to ITRU to discuss some potential problems in training. The new system entailed classifying, coding, and recording the consignments; it necessitated a primary sorting into a number of different storage areas, consulting a console about the availability of storage bins, and retrieving consignments by making use of the recorded information when delivery was called for.

The contrast between the demands on the men under the old system and under the new was sharp. Under the old system, the men physically manhandled parcels into some appropriate storage area and recorded the details on one of their documents. Many of their problems sprang from original paperwork errors (one or two parcels in a consignment might fail to make the plane, even though they were recorded as being on the flight delivery, for example). Other problems were attributable in part to the difficulties of coping with items which were physically very dissimilar in spite of belonging to a single consignment from one firm to another. Small parcels would be withdrawn for storage in a small parcels area and long items would go to another. Valuables needed special storage, and so on. There was even a special cold-room for coffins, a surprising indication of the vogue amongst Irish Americans for being buried in dear old Ireland. But the cargo handlers could always check that they were helping themselves to the right item when one of the collectors called for his goods by making a personal search and inspecting the labels on the parcels in the various storage areas. The search could be assisted by the handler 'remembering' where the parcel was, or by consulting another handler who might help when a parcel was hard to locate. Difficulties sometimes arose because the contents of one storage area would spill over into another, or because an item taken out in error would not be returned, or because one item within a consignment might be stored for physical reasons in a different place from the other items. Certainly, search took up a fair proportion of a handler's time, much of it being spent in looking for things lost. Orderliness was not altogether helped by the belief of some impatient collectors that the operation could be assisted by a tip.

What made the new system so different in its human demands was the removal of *looking* as the key to retrieval. Parcels were to be held in multi-storey decks divided by a narrow passage which was not normally open to access. The crane which travelled in the passage could be operated manually, but it was designed to move automatically through remote control by the console operator. The potential problem with the new system was its low tolerance of mistakes. If an item was not where it was supposed to be, it could only be retrieved by a Sherlock Holmes, and certainly not by a spate of activity or feat of memory. The skills of the new system emphasized tidy-mindedness, accuracy of thinking, and recording and analytical ability. These were not the obvious qualities to be expected from the robust, good-humoured but down-to-earth cargo-handlers, most of whom came from simple rural backgrounds.

If there were grounds for taking a none too optimistic view of the prospects, there was added cause for concern from experiences elsewhere. There had already been resistance to correct procedures in operating the terminal in two large airports in Europe; and in one the system had undergone a temporary collapse. Nor was the trouble confined to Europe. In one location in the State of New York, the loaders had developed a predilection for by-passing the console and using the crane manually to search for and to withdraw consignments from the storage areas in the multi-storage decks: so it became a re-enactment of the old system in a new setting.

Here then were all the ingredients for some future dispute: the economics of operation called for sudden change; expensive equipment, once installed, could not stay idle for long; nor could two methods of warehousing run in parallel without creating double confusion. There was little room for sweeteners in the form of wage increases, without destroying the delicate balance of wage differentials amongst the remaining jobs at the airport. To make matters more difficult, Irish trade unions are amongst the most militant in Europe, as a study of the international statistics relating to industrial disputes will reveal, although this was partly counterbalanced by the progressive record of Aer Lingus, which with its international connections had long been in the forefront of new thinking in management.

Operators assess new system before training

The best hope for resolving the human and technical problems lay in enlisting the support of the men and treating the whole operation as an adventure. Out of necessity, training had to start before the equipment arrived and with many details still to be settled about how each job was to be performed and about which people should do which jobs. The dilemma was this: if a system had not been finalized, how does training begin?

After much deliberation and quandary, the outcome was to train the men to perform all the jobs, and to introduce them to a wide range of operating problems, irrespective of whether or not these problems had been fully resolved by the industrial and planning engineers. In effect, the men were being challenged to investigate the mysteries of the future. Manual workers accustomed to limited responsibilities were being asked to take a hand in furthering their own skill by developing a comprehensive understanding of a system that was not yet in being. The principles being applied here were those which had been developed in the course of international demonstration programmes in the training of older workers and embodied in an approach known as the 'Discovery Method' of training. In this case, the method, which sets out to elicit positive thought in mastering a skill, had an additional end in view. Its purpose was not simply to facilitate understanding but also to act as a medium for the promotion of attitude change towards working methods.

Effectiveness much depends on the trainer. The choice fell on Mick Costello, by nature a catalytic personality with a capacity for carrying people with him. He set out to gain the support and interest of the loaders by giving them the opportunity to fly over to Amsterdam where they could see the new equipment in use. They returned full of lively comments and criticisms.

The senior loaders were then invited into a training class. The rudiments of the new system were re-stated, and they were then asked: 'What do you think the problems are going to be?' 'That's what you're supposed to be telling us,' Mick Costello was told. After a while, it dawned on the participants that if they had come to expect answers they were not going to get them. At the end of the session, all the trainees dispersed with an air of disillusionment. Mick thought he had overdone it. But the following day they were back again. This time they poured out not only snags and difficulties but suggestions on how they might be overcome. They debated and argued amongst themselves. But occasionally they would refer a point to the instructor, who always managed to keep one jump ahead. At the end of several sessions, and when most of their recommendations had been finalized, Mick came to the fore again with an account of the way in which it had been envisaged that the new system might best operate. It corresponded with what the senior loaders, with promptings, had proposed.

The new system called for great accuracy with documentation and while this could be most readily learned by following a job through under actual conditions, acquisition of the appropriate mental skills did not entirely depend on the physical presence of the equipment and of the parcels. Simulation was easy. Actual parcels were replaced by wooden models, each being inscribed with the dimensions of the larger 'real' parcels represented. The documents themselves were real, but training entries were made up to allow the trainees ample experience in dealing with a full range of problem items and documentation errors. The availability of storage bins and the use of information from the console lent itself to a game which could be played by two men with a pack of training cards.

Solving the problems, working on the exercises, and playing the game, gave the trainees ample opportunity for self-expression. The lessons were soon passed on informally among the men and when the next batch of loaders presented themselves for training, it was clear that they were not complete novices.

A few of the cargo loaders put up a somewhat hesitant performance in training and the odd man gave vent to his self-doubts. This, plus the deferment of the scheduled starting time of the new system due to late delivery of the equipment, suggested that it might be desirable to arrange a refresher check before 'D-day'. But how was this to be done? The solution was to arrange an examination-type questionnaire, the completion of which was voluntary. However, those who gained more than a stipulated mark became eligible for a money prize based on a lucky draw. The response was overwhelming and led to bits of personal coaching where a loader was revealed as misinformed.

In due course, the vast new mechanized warehouse was completed, the equipment installed and tested, and the moment for change-over from one system to another had arrived. One busy weekend was spent in moving all cargo into the new terminal. Then on the Monday morning the old system gave place to the new. Whatever the snags were in the new system—there were many teething troubles as there always are—none of them concerned the behaviour and performance of the cargo-handlers. The smoothness of the transfer earned high praise from the management of Aer Lingus and led to a re-enactment of the project for inclusion in an American film on retraining, called 'Live and Learn'.

The retraining project at Dublin Airport, while it had many informal aspects, was based on careful planning. The men had been involved from the outset and the incorporation of discovery learning allowed them to appraise for themselves the problems which the new storage system would present. The greatest area of uncertainty was the contribution which the loaders would make in helping to ensure that the project moved in the right direction. In fact, the men responded, contributed positive suggestions, developed their skills, and subsequently identified themselves with the success of the whole operation.

GUIDE TO ACTION

The instructor who sets out to teach something to adult trainees will never be far away from the problem of how to motivate them. But once people decide on a goal for themselves and take a hand in organizing their own learning, his task is largely one of channelling their efforts in the right direction. If one of the objectives of training is to encourage people to show initiative in work, then the first step must be to encourage them to show initiative in organizing their own learning. How can this be done?

Self-belief

Adults must believe in themselves as learners and each should be encouraged to relate this concept to the image he holds of himself.

The greatest barrier to training arises from people believing that learning is not for them. This feeling may be countered by encouraging them to engage in any form of further education however different the content may be from that which is to be covered in training. After discovering that they *have* learned, adults begin to see themselves as learners. Those who have worked with middle-aged trainees are impressed by the enthusiasm which they subsequently display for the whole process of learning.

Stimulation by challenge

Adults are demotivated when they believe that they are entering into an area which is clearly defined and the elements of which merely need to be transferred to them in some mechanical way. The converse feeling is created when they are introduced to some element of mystery, to some interesting problem that needs to be solved. Even in areas of certainty, a challenge can be created. The design of training can incorporate fields which centre round problems or projects in which the trainees are deliberately starved of information. The trainees search for and learn to extract the information they need. The process can be given added meaning where different search requirements are placed on different individuals. Where collective effort is required, each trainee can be encouraged to acquaint himself fully with one aspect of the course, so that in that particular aspect he can be better informed than his colleagues.

Reconciling control and freedom

Adults continue to learn while they can see that they are making progress, but they are loth to allow their rate of progress to be publicized so that it can be compared with that of others. Conditions which favour self-improvement must enable learners to check easily that they are progressing in the right direction. This information will be more readily acceptable if it can be kept private. Teaching machines which pass on to the next frame only when the knob relating to the correct answer is pressed; question and answer cards which contain the question on one side and the answer on the other; automated class rooms which enable the aggregate answers from pupils to be available to the teacher without identifying the contributors and which allow the teacher to proceed at the right pace for all members of the class; and finally self-marking and self-assessment; these are amongst the methods that bridge the gap between the need for controlled progress and a recognition of the adult's desire to maintain his sense of personal freedom and identity during learning.

7. Strategies in Review

Our primary concern at ITRU is to consider how training can best be designed to enable trainees to acquire skills and knowledge in industrial operations. Where the recipients are mature adults, a whole set of special features demand additional treatment as they relate to the conditions, the emphasis, the atmosphere and the strategy of approach to training. Some of these have been touched on in our Guides to Action, but there are certain subjects that transcend chapter boundaries.

1. REDUCING TENSION

Adult learners who can be helped over the difficult early stages are likely to make steady progress and to have a longer life within the firm after training than younger trainees. This is one of the findings of an ITRU study of adults in training.* Yet many firms are more conscious of initial difficulties than of any ultimate benefits.

Men and women with a tendency to become overwrought are likely to display conspicuous anxiety at the outset of employment. Some companies use the assessment of anxiety as a criterion for discrimination at selection. The personnel manager of one large departmental store placed his employees on a variety of jobs for very brief periods to assess their suitability for promotion. Those who showed symptoms of fear or tension

---

* Newsham, D. B. *The Challenge of Change to the Adult Trainee*. Training Information Paper No. 3. London: HMSO, 1969.

were sacked on the grounds that they could not adjust to change; the others were promoted. Another company regularly used a personality inventory as a more formal method of discriminating against anxious trainees. And, as shown in Chapter 1, yet another company's representative rejected anyone who looked anxious on seeing the training manual at interview. It is little wonder that where personality tests are used in the selection of candidates for responsible positions, it is commonly found that applicants fake responses away from neuroticism in the direction of stability. The irony is that for some jobs, anxious people can rank amongst the best prospects. Evidence collected by ITRU suggests, for example, that this is the case with industrial foremen: those rated highly by one large corporation were more anxious than those with middle or lower ratings. The weakness of using anxiety as a criterion for sifting out the less promising is well expressed by the adage:

> 'A highly anxious employee who makes mature responses to his problem is more effective than the less anxious person who makes immature ones.'

There may therefore be some merit in recruiting an applicant who shows signs of being anxious and concerned about the job but is suitable on general grounds.

Even so, anxiety does have a spoiling effect on an older person's progress in learning. One principal has illustrated this by declaring that on weekend courses for supervisors run in his technical college there will be at least one man off before each Sunday night with a psychosomatic disorder. This, he maintains, is because the firm supplying the recruits 'springs it' on the men at the last minute and there is no time on a short course to calm them. Anxiety can also turn men and women into most difficult people to handle. An instructor in British Rail who was concerned with retraining men from mechanical to electrical operations said:

> 'Men over 50 are frightened of anything new and are chary of applying for promotion if it requires new learning. The

new electrical signals are twenty times easier to control, but the older man thinks that mentally it will be too much for him. Men change from being calm, at ease, and relaxed to being so tense you dare not go near them.'

As a means of counterbalancing any tendency to over-anxiety, there are several steps that a training officer can take to protect his trainee. These are discussed below.

Social support

The famous Russian physiologist Pavlov used to find in his experimental studies on the behaviour of sheep that having a second sheep in the room had a calming effect on the first sheep. The 'social sheep' is not without its parallels in human society. People need the support of others when they are unsure of themselves. It is of interest to note here that a group of students on correspondence courses preparatory to application to the Open University put in a special plea for contact with other students. 'If only we knew how other people were doing we would feel better. Are we really behindhand? Are we up to average? Do other adults find the same problems as we do? Am I alone in my worries?' These are the questions which were obsessing them during the course of their solitary studies.

Social support is also important during recruitment. Some companies have found it easier to recruit older women by canvassing and holding meetings in local rooms, whether in urban neighbourhoods or villages, than by resorting to conventional means of individual recruitment at headquarters. In the case of retraining within a company the task is easier as the groups already exist. The now well-publicized case histories of adult conversion training—the SPEAR project at Steel Peach & Tozer, Churchmans' training of maintenance operators for the cigar factory, and so on—may owe much to the existence of pre-formed social groups which were inherent in their conversion programmes.

Once trainees have been recruited, social support becomes important again in providing the conditions for continued progress. In the highly successful factory at Bargoed (see Chapter 5, Part 3) almost all the employees lived in the same valley, had the same background (mining) and the same handicap (pneumonoconiosis). Social bonds developed spontaneously and with great effect. Such examples are a rarity because in modern industrial communities few people have very much in common. Individuals usually need encouragement to form groups, especially when they are middle-aged. They will often admit mistrust as to whether they are going to be acceptable to others, especially to younger people. Older trainees, however, have a relatively good performance record and a low leaving rate in the developing environment of a new factory. Here they can participate on equal terms in the establishment of work standards and in the formation of social groups.

Where there is no positive basis for group cohesion, there is something to be said for inviting trainees to contribute to training course design or to have a say in the content. It is all a matter of degree. If too much is left unstructured there is a danger that anxieties could be multiplied rather than reduced. On the other hand, a certain amount of trainee discretion in a limited field could promote interaction between members of a group. This is something that cannot be rushed. A show of hands on issues of two short breaks versus one long break hardly assists group formation. The discretionary area must be one which is left open for a sufficient period to allow people to engage in a discussion of adequate depth amongst themselves, and is probably best conducted outside the immediate training environment. An example has been cited in the Aer Lingus study in Chapter 6, Part 5.

When large-scale technological changes are taking place in industry the major challenge for those working in Personnel does not always lie in the new level of skill demanded. Many skills seemingly beyond the accomplishment of unskilled workers can develop rapidly in a favourable social climate. This is where the much neglected social learning of groups has a special role to play.

An acceptable instructor

Schoolchildren take it as a matter of course that some of their teachers will be good and others will be bad. So it seems to be with the adult trainee's assessment of instructors, except that an adult, unlike a schoolchild, is not obliged to endure a poorly-regarded teacher. An adult can quit without being accused of truancy, and he is much better placed than a schoolchild for 'answering back'.

Much of the evidence on what constitutes a good instructor of adults comes from the comments which adult trainees make about those who teach them. In one respect at least their comments run counter to common opinion. This concerns the age of their instructors. It is usually supposed that middle-aged trainees require older men as their teachers, but in many cases trainees have spoken in most appreciative terms of instructors who were younger than themselves. The younger instructor often has several advantages. Being conscious of the status inversion, he is very much on his guard to treat his trainees with deference and respect. And, being nearer to the experience of learning the skill, he tends to show greater insight into their problems. 'Age doesn't matter as long as he doesn't make you feel small because you don't know as much as he does', was one trainee's comment. The older learner has a tremendous amount of experience and know-how gained over the years, and if the younger instructor, while lacking this, has the compensating advantage of special knowledge, they will very nearly be on equal terms in status and relationship.

Curiously, older instructors appear to be favoured more by young trainees, perhaps because of their father-figure image. The most consistent objection to younger instructors seems to relate not so much to youthfulness as to problems of role relationship created by previous acquaintance. 'We aren't going to be told what to do by young so-and-so when we've know her since she was in her cradle', was one of the relatively rare objections to a younger instructor, and, no doubt, a legacy of small-town recruitment.

Perhaps the most important attribute of the instructor of adults, regardless of age, is the notion that he is 'one of the group'. In two of the case studies, the instructor had come from the same background as the trainees—an ex-railwayman in a factory teaching ex-railwaymen to become roller bearing inspectors; an ex-miner in another factory teaching ex-miners to work in a car factory. In the case studies quoted from the U.S.A., two of the most successful instructors were negroes (teaching negroes). One of them in fact had previously ranked amongst the 'disadvantaged'. The adult trainee seems to look at his instructor as an ally, rather than as a model, and he seeks in him the qualities that are sought in friendship. He seems to be looking for an acceptable person and a sensitive communicator rather than a master craftsman.

In a number of field experiments carried out by ITRU, the choice of instructors has confounded normal conventions and might be rationalized by the adage 'It may be easier to train a teacher in the skill to be taught than to teach a craftsman how to teach'. The craftsman often has difficulty in distinguishing between the practice of a skill and the practice of teaching and sometimes it is the former which remains the focal point of his orientation. His belief in natural aptitude and the value of long experience will render him an unwilling convert to the psychology of learning and to the professionalism of training. The instructor picked for his valuable qualities as a teacher, on the other hand, is obliged by his very ignorance to apply himself to an analytical diagnosis of the skill and to re-interpret all that he discovers in terms of the learning process. The instructor can therefore be primarily a craftsman or a teacher, a performer or a communicator. The priority we give to the instructor as a communicator rests with his ability to impart the content of the skill in an efficient fashion; but equally important is his capacity for personal and social communication. Adults as trainees are likely to be a more variable group than juveniles, and while an insensitive rule-of-thumb approach might 'get by' with young trainees it will almost

certainly fail with those who are older. If the instructor of
adults succeeds in creating the right atmosphere and helping
to bring about a real dialogue with his trainees, he is well on
the road to success.

A secure future

Using conventional criteria, the most successful in-firm training schemes are those in which the trainees are guaranteed
the jobs for which they are being trained at the end of their
training. Where 'failures' are precluded, trainees seem more
willing to learn. Being more confident about securing a given
job at the end of their training, they apply themselves with
the sense of adventure found in those embarking on a second
career. Training is an experience to be enjoyed, and trainees
perform all the better for it. An added advantage of the
guaranteed future is the peculiar effect which this has on the
way in which the instructor goes about his job. He is dis-
inclined to engage in moral judgments about the quality of
his trainees, since he has no easy let-out by failing the weaker
members. All his energies are directed towards ensuring that
he meets their problems wherever they may lie. He knows,
too, that management will assess him solely on the results of
his teaching.

The picture we are presenting of adult trainees contrasts
sharply with the outsider's view, i.e. that the mature adult
trainee will apply himself most effectively when he has the
incentive of a job as the bait before him. This 'economic'
picture of the adult trainee misrepresents his psychology. It is
not uncommon for adult trainees to withdraw completely before taking their final test when their success seemed assured.
The consideration of 'we will give you an extension of training to try again if you fail' has no calming effect. And where
adults do fail, instructors often remark that the trainees talk
themselves into failure. It is interesting to note that during
ITRU's work with London Transport in the training of bus
drivers, one instructor with the most successful record of

teaching older men declared: 'I never mention the word "fail". I always act as though I know they're going to pass'.

It is not surprising to psychologists that there are conditions where high incentive produces poorer performance than low incentive. Motivation requires an optimal level of arousal. The adult trainee, usually long deprived of training or educational experience, is certainly aroused by the stimulating conditions which he finds in training. His problem is usually not one of under-arousal but of over-arousal. Too much arousal (i.e. too high an incentive) produces an overload of anxiety and often a breakdown in his performance.

At the time of ITRU's research exercises at the London Postal School, a trainee could be dismissed at the end of training through failure to pass the final examination. An older man had sometimes relinquished another job because of his ambition to work in the Post Office and had passed through a set of selection tests. As training proceeded, anxieties would mount. Not only might he not secure the desired job, but he would probably not get back his old job. The dismissed trainee enjoys no redundancy gratuity and he has least claim on an employer. His prestige, too, is at stake. 'I'm not waiting to fail the test. I've never had the sack yet. I'd rather leave of my own accord.' This kind of remark was repeated by a number of older men who, according to their instructor, stood every chance of passing. They either left before the first test or declined a second chance with an extension of training time. Such a decision also revoked their claim to unemployment benefit.

An example might also be quoted of one of 'the most intelligent personnel' who was offered day release from a chemical firm in preparation for a City and Guilds examination. This man passed his first year examination and towards the end of the second year left—not the classes, but the firm. His explanation was '... I was just scared of not passing the second year examination or of falling behind the others. You see, I've been a leading hand and I've a reputation to keep up. I might fail to do so'.

It is useful then for a company to weigh up the relative pros and cons of guaranteeing employment on completion of a course of training. The risk may be far less than is generally supposed if protection against the bad employee is sought not by a final test or examination but by a screening test at entrance. ITRU has been active in this field in developing trainability tests to check whether applicants have an adequate capacity for engaging in the form of learning that is required.* These tests have shown themselves to be of greatest value with middle-aged and older applicants. If the applicant is assessed as capable of learning, it is incumbent on the training organization to ensure that he reaches the requisite standard of performance. Nothing that has been said, however, argues against the notion of a final test as a measure of attainment or as a means whereby the training department can check its own efficiency. But it is where the final test is used as the discriminator and arbiter of ultimate employment that we see a real threat both to the security and performance of the adult trainee.

2. CREATING AN ADULT ATMOSPHERE

One of the most common remarks one hears from adults contemplating training is that it means going back to school. To the pessimist, learning is often seen as a regressive experience rather than as an exciting opening to a second career, an impression which is reinforced by the way in which much adult training is conducted—in an old-fashioned classroom style. 'I'm writing this down,' said one 60-year-old steam train driver, copying notes from the blackboard on the use of electricity, 'but I don't know what the hell I'm writing about'. On other occasions, an atmosphere may be developed that is more appropriate for handling an unruly class in a secondary school. In one large clothing company, trainees—young and old—were cautioned against talking during the practical work of training and, if they persisted, the piped music was

* *See* Downs, S. 'Predicting training potential'. *Personnel Management*, **2**, 26–8, 1970.

turned off. In another firm, when work was interrupted due to a shortage of components from a production department, the trainees were told, 'Don't just sit there, find *something* to do, or at least *look* as if you're working'. In these firms a common complaint was of the 'adolescent discipline'.

A similar theme was found when an ITRU research team interviewed trainees who had left organizations before the end of their training. Feeling ran high against one instructor who, it was said, kept a trainee for thirty minutes making him explain why he had been five minutes late; 'When you don't live in the area and you have to change buses twice it's not easy to be punctual'. 'The trouble with the instructor is that he treated us like children' was one comment that had many variants. On this score, adult trainees are reluctant to make concessions.

There are small incidental things too that seem to create a poor impression. The reluctance to fill in an application form might be accounted for by illiteracy except that this reluctance is also shown by those who are quite adequately literate. People react against questions that embarrass or miss the point. The married woman applicant who is returning to industry after twenty years finds it degrading to register that her last salary was £4 per week. She also muses on the attitude her interviewer will take to 'Hobbies—None'. Should she admit that as a middle-aged woman she has no outdoor activities? Or do they expect her to have some—as well as four children to rear?

Another factor which affects the sense of adult atmosphere is the age composition of the training groups. An older adult feels isolated if surrounded by teenagers and seldom survives the training period. But where training groups are composed solely of older trainees, including one or two who are regarded as elderly, there is an equally unfavourable reaction by the younger members to being placed among the 'old crocks'. A sprinkling of younger trainees, however, gives reassurance that older trainees are not being treated as a special or disadvantaged group.

One instructor, observing the value of having young and older trainees working together, expressed the advantages as follows, 'The young often find themselves stuck on what they should do next. Rather than come back to the instructor—and in so doing appear not to have learned—they would rather go to the older students to ask "what was it he said we had to do after this?"'. The older trainees, for their part, gain confidence from being consulted. A student aged 50, a grandmother, said: 'I find examinations difficult, and here the younger students can help me with advice. But I also find some of the students come to me with their problems, mostly emotional, in a way they would not go to a lecturer'. This relationship helps the self-esteem of the mature students and counterbalances any difficulties arising from sitting with people half their age.

Whether this interpretation is correct or not, a study in a catering establishment and another in the Post Office* discount the belief that adults should be trained within their own age groups. In the Post Office, both younger and older men passed out of the training school more quickly when they were trained in mixed age groups than when trained separately; with the catering staff it seemed to be the younger recruits who benefited most by working with the older. In support of these combined findings is the conclusion of an international working party on the employment of older workers that older trainees perform better when trained in mixed age groups than when trained together. If a class of adults needs to be divided into groups, their previous educational experience forms a better basis than age.

Creating the right atmosphere for adult training depends also on the very material and content of training. Drucker** quotes the case of a Dutch convent which recruited middle-aged women, many of them widows of 50 or so, as candidates to their teaching order. Only one of a large number survived

---

* ITRU. 'Should older recruits be trained separately?'. Research Note in *Industrial and Commercial Training*, **1**, No. 2, 63, 1969.
** Drucker, Peter F. 'The knowledge society'. *New Society*, pp. 629-31, April 1969.

the probation period to take her vows. She, when asked why the others had left, replied that all the applicants had to start by taking a course in sewing, an activity which many of them had been doing on behalf of their children, nephews or nieces for most of their adult lives. 'If we had wanted to sew, we would have stayed where we were'. It is evident that adult trainees have a clear idea of what they think constitutes a fit and proper form of training.

Not only must training meet a standard of relevance and competence but a standard of acceptability too. At the Bargoed factory described earlier, which had originally been set up to make toy cars before switching predominantly to work for the motor trade, there was a great reluctance amongst trainees to learn on the toy components. One instructor said: 'If it's soldering they have to learn, then they like to learn on production parts, even if there is no difference in the type of soldering performed'. Where there are striking differences between training material and production material the resistance is stronger still. This was apparent amongst adult trainees in a company manufacturing dresses. An instructor declared: 'We daren't drill them on paper or bonded fibre—they think it degrading'.

When mature adults are the trainees, there are limiting factors of a psychological nature governing training design. On the one hand there is a need to overcome lack of confidence by giving them easy tasks within their accomplishment but, on the other, the instructor has to avoid making the tasks look infantile. Giving a less able or more anxious trainee a simpler task than his fellows runs the risk of reducing his sense of adult status. So too does lowering the standards of acceptance. All this requires most careful handling. The instructor may do best in striving to retain the adult atmosphere even at the expense of some technical loss in training efficiency.

For all this, maintaining an adult atmosphere is not simply a matter of bolstering the trainee's ego by offering him the preferential treatment denied to juveniles or protecting his self-esteem by ensuring that he is not given things he considers beneath him. In a positive sense, it means striving to build up the climate of the class to take account of the full maturity latent within it. This maturity of outlook is reflected in common utterances heard from both trainees and instructors. Characteristic comments from some British Rail trainees included: 'If we ask questions it is because we want to gain confidence. We want to know whether we are going the right way or not'; 'I refuse to remember without understanding'. These comments suggest a reason why some adults take longer in training. They set themselves a standard of attainment which may be higher than that asked of them. Not content merely to familiarize themselves with the training material, they seek to get on top of it. This striving of adults to use their full maturity is reflected too in the comments of instructors. One in a Government Training Centre put it this way: 'Younger men lack the diagnostic ability of the older and often do not adequately finish the work.'

In refashioning the course material to suit adults, the opportunity is there to open up fresh standards of attainment. Mature students are capable of going beyond a basic course and the notion that they are being kept down to an elementary level is prejudicial to their performance and morale.

3. ARRANGING THE SCHEDULE

Most schedules of training are planned with young trainees in mind and are seldom modified to take account of an adult intake. School leavers with many years of recent schooling are still adjusted to the discipline of the classroom, and usually fit in with whatever programme is arranged. There is no faster way of becoming aware of the special needs that adults impose on the training timetable than by a sudden switch from juvenile to mature trainees.

Adult induction courses

The first indication of these special problems is the realization that an orthodox programme often cannot begin on time, or, if it does, it is likely to suffer from a bad start. It is not an opportune moment to begin to teach complex skills when trainees are preoccupied with the fact of starting, with the details of their new environment, and with meeting their instructors and colleagues. Objectively, the situation is the same for juveniles and adults, but the two situations can be treated as effectively different. Juveniles are usually content to meet people and to learn at the same time, while adults prefer to do one thing at a time.

The biggest difference, perhaps, concerns the attitude of trainees to the job itself and to the training as a means of job entry. The juvenile will often put off thoughts about the ultimate, preferring to reserve judgment until he gets to it, and will concentrate on the immediate situation. The adult trainee is far more inclined to see the training as a means to an end and to be continually relating in his mind the demands of the actual job and the nature of the training being provided to meet those demands.

Because of these differences, it is often advisable to provide some job familiarization for the adult starter in spite of contrary pointers from juveniles who are inclined to view such preliminaries as a waste of time. For the adult trainee, however, the advantages might be listed as follows:

1. He is given a chance to ensure that the realities of the job correspond with his ideas about it. This materially increases the prospect of his staying if he completes his training.

   A fair number of older adults interviewed because they left their jobs soon after training have expressed disillusion. 'I never thought all those selection tests and medical exams would lead me to a job like this.'

2. By seeing the actual demands of everyday work, he finds it easier to absorb the training and to translate abstract or general points into concrete terms.

3. Through observing the live situation, perhaps in an ancillary role, he is more likely to cast off apprehensions about

the job that interfere with progress during training. ITRU learnt from a manager in one factory that older trainees were so terrified of the large and unfamiliar machines that they stood against the walls, fearing an explosion! Another manager in a cement processing plant said of his recruits: 'One look at that enormous panel of flashing lights and dials just frightens them away.'

Fears seem to be allayed, however, when trainees enter into the work situation in a non-training role. It also helps when trainees are able to observe: 'That chap says he's only been here three weeks. If he can do that after three weeks I'm sure I can.'

In one company, trainees explored some expensive and complex equipment when it was 'cold', i.e. not running, and this gave them a good deal of encouragement on a machine which was noisy and formidable during operation. More common examples are of trainees spending a probationary period on the machine in a servicing capacity as a feeder or labourer.

An interesting example of an induction period to a training course is provided by the Labour Directorate under the Norwegian Ministry of Labour. This has a successful record of recruiting and training adults over a wide age span, mostly drawn from the unskilled group and often with an agricultural background, for service in the Merchant Marine. While much of the training is more conveniently carried out in the classroom or practical class, a start is always made in a seagoing ship. This gives the trainees an intimate picture of what life at sea is really like. During this period, the instructors maintain the discipline that obtains at sea, use nautical jargon and expect trainees to do the same. Those who at this stage do not find the way of life to their liking, or who are slow to adapt to their new environment, normally drop out from the course. In fact, few participants leave and between 85 and 90 per cent of those who complete the course take up employment at sea. The largest 'long-serving' groups of retrained men are found amongst those who were the oldest trainees.

An example of a well-received induction period in one of ITRU's field experiments comes from work with London Transport in the training of bus drivers. For a trainee who has never driven a car it is a frightening exerience to start driving a bulky bus through London traffic, which is the way in which training courses normally began. Instead, ITRU developed an off-the-road bus track and a series of exercises and tasks. Trainees were able to acquire the manipulative skills of bus driving without risk of collision and were even allowed to drive a bus around without having an instructor in it. It was the older trainees who gained most benefit from this preliminary training.

Staggering the intake

Since the induction period is by its very nature undemanding on instruction time it serves to keep trainees occupied when instructors are busy. Hence trainees can be enrolled and started even if the training department is not ready for them. Promising recruits need never be turned away. Government Training Centres, by staggering intake, have been able to reduce waiting time for a training place amongst those out of work. But here our main point is not economic nor social nor one of administrative convenience. Staggering the intake carries a training advantage. The mature adult trainee is encouraged to see that others, a week or two ahead of him, are progressing and have settled down. A staggered intake creates the impression that people are being taken on and are getting somewhere; that they are joining a process that has a visibly successful outcome. It allows comparisons to be made of a type that stimulates interest, and encourages emulation. But *competitive* comparisons with all the anxieties associated with them are avoided. The 'staggered' principle can be usefully extended further into training. Performing exercises in a different order disguises from the class members the different rates of progress that each trainee makes. The decision of whether or not to base training on a staggered intake is one of some consequence. If the principle is accepted, some revision of schedules will be necessary to allow for flexibility within the programme.

Length of practical sessions

The next step in modifying an orthodox training programme concerns the grouping and spacing of training material. With younger trainees, there are problems of holding their attention. In consequence, the timetable is inclined to become punctuated with short breaks, pep talks, items of interest, and visits outside the training school. Younger trainees often like to move on rapidly to later items in the programme, being impatient if they believe that they are being held back. For them, variety is the spice of life and a key factor in maintaining the dynamism of the course.

In contrast, mature adult trainees tend to be aggravated if dragged away for diversionary activities from the set tasks on which they have been working. Typical comments are: 'I like to accomplish one thing at a time', and 'I like to get the feel of a target'. The mature adult trainee often lingers on when the class has broken up, and is not averse to maintaining his activity by providing his own homework. During experiments at the London Postal School, many of the older trainees would take away lists of the street names and the postal areas of London to learn, and would return next day telling how their wives had tested them on packs of cards they had made themselves.

Contrary to many existing beliefs, mature adults also seem to learn better with long sessions. This is not to say that they necessarily need *more* training time. Mature trainee teachers in an experiment which ITRU conducted at Garnett College, for example, were found to do better with five two-hour sessions than with ten one-hour periods when learning from a teaching machine. The young trainees, however, had exactly the opposite preference*. This tendency for older trainees to achieve better results with relatively long learning periods has been confirmed in experiments both with manual letter sorting and with women learning to mend worsted cloth invisibly**.

The adult's susceptibility to annoyance when a venture is interrupted is based on a simple psychological fact. Interruption causes forgetting, and this is true when the learning has not been consolidated. In fact, the effects of interference on short term memory increase with age. The middle-aged woman who was learning to be a clerk typist might have done far better if she had structured her own course: '...just as we've worked out our typewriting tabulation we have to go off to an English lesson and when we come back we have to start all over again with working out the tabulation'.

Older trainees admit their occasional inability to concentrate: 'My concentration is all right unless I get tired by jobs at home—then I lose track of the instructor'. Yet they will often reject the idea of a 'break'.

There are various ways of relieving the tedium of a long training session other than by engaging in diversionary activity. For example, older adults enjoy working in pairs. Setting each other questions, timing each other, or even discussing their common difficulties all provide a break from formal learning while at the same time giving the appearance of continuity. Another possibility is allowing changes to revolve round method rather than round content. A change of method (say from vocal to visual or from learning to self-testing and so on) can enrich appreciation of the matter being learned. On the other hand, change in content seems to produce in mature trainees a sense of the need to wipe the slate clean.

---

* *See* Neale, J. G., Toye, M. H., and Belbin, E. 'Adult training: the use of programmed instruction'. *Occupational Psychology*, **42**, 23–31, 1968.
** *See* Belbin, E. *Training the Adult Worker*. Problems of Progress in Industry, No. 15. London: HMSO, 1964.

Whole or part method?

These observations bear on the issue of whole or part techniques in training mature learners. In general, older learners prefer a whole method. 'It's better to understand what you're doing than to get the right answer', said one older trainee philosophically. One instructor in a Government Training Centre commented 'older people conceptualize. They *appear* to be going slowly, but this is only while they get an overall grasp of what they have to do.' In contrast, he said that youngsters branch off on some detail and then find themselves stuck on what to do next. If an older learner can be helped to form an overall view, his learning is likely to be hastened. But the very nature of some tasks excludes them from being learned by whole methods. In such cases a cumulative part method has advantages over the progressive part method. The latter method divides the material into small, easy sections that are learned one at a time and usually works well with younger trainees. The cumulative part method is similar but here each of the parts is combined as training proceeds—a, $a + b$, $a + b + c$, and so on. Thus the new parts do not interfere with memory of the old. The old parts are retained and consolidated while the new are learned. A well designed training task can ensure that parts a and b, which by this method are practised most frequently, are in fact those which require most practice.

Starting slowly

A trainee learning spoolwinding in a textile firm said:

> 'The job wasn't so much difficult as impossible to do in the time allotted. We just weren't given enough time to learn and we were expected to be on production and we couldn't earn production bonuses in anything like the time they gave us and we felt very sore about it. Some of us just couldn't take this and left. We felt like leaving too, but we stuck it and finally mastered it.'

The fastest learner is not always the most successful performer on the job. One firm manufacturing agricultural
fertilizers selected thirteen of its men for training as process
operators on its new automated plant. Their ages ranged from
27 to 59, with the oldest member being by far the slowest
learner. His progress was hindered by the fact that he tried
to test everything against the background of his former experience in a desire to master the know-how of the plant. Now
as an established operator, he is one of three out of the thirteen
to be ranked as 'outstanding' on a five-point scale.

Another programme to teach train drivers to become bus
drivers stipulated a three-week training period. Very few of
the over 50s passed. But 93 per cent of them passed when the
training time was extended to seven weeks.

A slow start with younger trainees often indicates a poor
ultimate performance, but the relationship is much less clear-
cut for those who are older.

4. CORRECTING ERRORS

Without the possibility or even the likelihood of error, training would be an unskilled art. The presumption that the
trainee is liable to go wrong lies at the heart of training. In
consequence, some policy must be adopted or practice followed for correcting mistakes. In the case of the adult trainee,
this is no simple matter.

For one thing, the adult trainee has a much higher measure
of commitment to the response he makes than the younger
trainee, because he tries to make certain that his action is
correct before engaging in it. During the early days of the
Nuffield Research Unit into Problems of Ageing, some of the
staff at Cambridge decided to make a very simple observa-
tional study of people posting letters. They stood outside the
post office in the centre of the town and recorded two things;
an estimate of the age of each person posting a letter and a
note on whether the letter was checked by a glance before
being posted. (This checking procedure in fact seemed quite

superfluous as no-one withdrew a letter as a result.) The findings of the study showed a striking relationship to age. Young people very seldom glanced at the address, older people invariably did so and the middle aged group fell in between.

In this type of activity there is no conflict between accuracy and anything else. Older people make certain that all is correct and this constitutes additional effort of their own choosing. In training, preoccupation with accuracy is sometimes bought at the expense of training time but not often in a way that produces any major problems. The exception is repetition work where accuracy has to be counterbalanced against the need to complete the task in the allotted time; here the passion for precision becomes a liability*.

The irony is that while older learners place a high premium on being correct they are almost as liable as younger learners to go wrong. Then, because they are so deliberate about what they do, 'reprogramming' becomes a more difficult operation. Laboratory studies of older learners have shown that as age rises, the tendency to repeat the same error increases. For example, in Professor H. Kay's experiments** on learning the relationship between a series of keys and a series of lights (by trial and error), older people showed a strong tendency to commit the same mistake many times in response to one particular light. So also in the experiments conducted by ITRU in the London Postal School, the trainee manual sorters were often disposed to place letters addressed to particular streets into the wrong district boxes on the sorting frame but were unwilling to believe that they were wrong. One trainee typified the problem by declaring while he incorrectly sorted some letters: 'I know that street goes into the NW1 box because I've lived in that area all my life'. He preferred to rationalize his behaviour rather than to make certain by looking. Eventually colour code marks were placed on the back of training pack letters in the school so that trainees could check through

* *See* Belbin, E. and Toye, M. H. 'Adult training: forcing the pace'. *Gerontology*, **1**, 33–7, 1970.
** Kay, H. 'Learning of a serial task by different age groups'. *Quarterly Journal of Experimental Psychology*, **3**, 166–83, 1951.

the sorted letters to see their own mistakes. This was found to be a more convincing and effective method for remedying errors than telling them that they were wrong.

Clearly, there are substantial gains in designing training in a way that allows trainees to spot their own mistakes before they become built into their habit patterns. But this is not always possible. Mistakes are committed and persist and one of the prime tasks of an instructor is to detect them and take appropriate action. How should he go about it? Does it follow from what has been said that immediate correction is the golden rule?

Time for correction

There are two fields of learning in which reporting back and correcting of error are better delayed. The first is in memorizing and the second is in conceptual learning.

First, let us look at errors in memorizing. ITRU gave postal sorters a task of remembering the counties in which some little-known hamlets were located.* It was found that telling them the correct county whenever they named the wrong one produced slower learning than telling them at the end of their test that they had made x errors. In both cases they were allowed to relearn after each test round of ten items. Immediate correction, then, can produce difficulties. These difficulties seem likely to be associated with the presence of interference factors which exercise such a disruptive effect on the ability to memorize as people age. The act of engaging in some other activity, however trivial, such as writing down a word in a short interval between learning something and recalling it, produces a disproportionate drop in retention amongst older people. It is the problem of holding something in mind while doing something else that seems increasingly difficult as people age. This is what the older postal sorters were being asked to do when they were given full information about their errors. They had the added

* *See* Downs, S. 'Mistakes in learning: effects on the older trainee'. *Industrial and Commercial Training*, **3**, 542-4, 1971.

overload of remembering what *not* to say next time round as well as what *to* say.

In correcting errors, instructors are doing two things of a very different character at the same moment. They are informing the trainee that he has made a mistake, which may have the effect of undermining self-confidence, and even the willingness to go on. They are also teaching him something which by its nature must present difficulties in learning, for otherwise he would have learned it correctly in the first instance.

Perhaps the best strategy which an instructor can adopt in such a case is to induce the trainee to correct himself in his own time and without jeopardy to his self-esteem.

Conceptual learning is the second field in which the reporting back of error needs to be handled judiciously and may be best delayed. But the reasons are somewhat different. A concept is usually structured over a period of time: it emerges both as a result of what a trainee learns in the training class and as a result of what he brings to the present from his past experience. In memorizing, one word can be substituted for another. By contrast, where learning involves comprehension, a wrong idea cannot simply be replaced by a right idea but usually requires a complete restructuring of concepts. Without this restructuring, learning becomes superficial and rootless.

The point may be illustrated by reference to driver training. A good driver is seldom one who automatically follows everything told him by his instructor; rather he is one who is essentially *developed* by his instructor. Unless the trainee is allowed to fashion his own ideas and have confidence in them, he is hardly likely to make a good driver. The best instructors help with this process. ITRU's work with London Transport has brought the moment of correction back from the point of occurrence amidst the traffic to the reconstruction of the trial drive over a model layout in the classroom. One used to hear: 'Check your speed. I said check your speed'. Rapidly changing traffic situations would prompt the bellowing out of abrupt instructions. There was little opportunity for the trainee, driving on a busy road, to determine exactly what was meant. (Did 'check your speed' mean braking? Or did it mean keeping the speed steady? Or did it mean, as one trainee thought, keeping his eyes on the speedometer?)

Reconstructing the drive round models in the classroom, however, provided an opportunity for the trainee to uncover the nature of his errors and to develop further his ideas about driving. The process proved valuable both because it allowed a degree of personal growth and because it gave the instructor a chance to learn about the trainee and about the concepts, correct or incorrect, which were underlying his sense of roadmanship. Often through question and answer, a way is found for overcoming the false notions that lie at the root of poor performance.

Overcoming errors committed during psycho-motor learning* poses yet another set of problems. As was shown in the case study of Mrs. Chatton, the sewing machinist (Chapter 3, Part 1), once she had picked up some wrong movements it was very difficult for her to discard them. This is an area in which immediate correction of error is justified and indeed essential before mistakes become consolidated to form habits. On many operations of this type, we need faster and more efficient methods for detecting errors and feeding back the information to the trainee. The ultimate is for a vigilant instructor to ensure that error is never allowed to creep into the trainee's repertoire, i.e. to ensure that the trainee acquires perfect technique and habits from the outset.

A final consideration concerns the relationship between correcting error and the trainee's own value system. The adult trainee tends to place a high store on accuracy over all other criteria of performance; to bring home all his mistakes is to affect him very deeply. A passion to get things right is both his great merit in the eyes of the employer and the kernel of

---

* Psycho-motor learning might be defined as learning to perform a repetitive set of high speed movements which have the character of acquired reflexes.

his self-esteem. When the adult trainee believes that he is making more than an isolated error he may be tempted to withdraw from the situation altogether.

5. INDIVIDUAL DIFFERENCES

Ageing is the great exaggerator of individual characteristics, especially those that have their roots in personality. With age, the amiable disposition becomes a model of benign serenity, the meticulous man an inflexible stickler, the reluctant learner a neurotic evader of everything that challenges the routine of life.

The enlargement of propensities is such that the instructor cannot fail to take them into account, for they have a real bearing on the type of teaching most likely to succeed.

The point was well illustrated when some new training methods were being developed to assist London Transport in teaching bus conductors to be drivers. Many were middle aged or born abroad. How could one best teach the man who had already learned to handle a bus and who was now adjusting himself to manoeuvring it correctly in complex traffic situations? Is it better for him to be guided through by being told exactly what to do in advance or is it better for the instructor to give his pupil his head? Not being sure, ITRU tried an experiment with both conditions and asked the pupils which method they preferred. The first trainee found it more helpful to have constant instruction provided he was in a situation which he had not fully mastered. The second trainee declared: 'I learn 100 per cent better on my own. Everyone has a different imagination. Sometimes the instructor thinks there will be an accident when I do not think so. I feel more confident when no-one is talking. You are not sure of yourself when you are being told all the time'.

Different instructional approaches

It requires a singularly sensitive instructor to perceive which key opens the door to learning. Most prefer to use a standard key and when the lock does not turn they see no need for self-reproach but refer to the inadequacy of their pupils. Again we turn to London Transport for an example of how important it is for an instructor to adjust himself to the individual demands of the trainees. With the help of the senior training staff and the Chief Examiner, we managed to isolate nine instructors out of a total of 116 who were conspicuously more successful or less successful in getting the trainees through the test. Each instructor was given a long interview by a member of ITRU who had no knowledge of the instructor's record with a view to finding out how he went about his task. All verbatim statements were later classified according to whether they were instructor-oriented, trainee-oriented or neutral. A statement was instructor-oriented if it drew attention to the instructor's teaching demands. A trainee-oriented statement comprised one in which the instructor intimated how he would mould his teaching to cope with particular problems of trainees. In classifying instructors by style and success rate the following picture emerged:

	Statements mainly:	
	Trainee-oriented	*Instructor-oriented*
Record of 116 instructors		
5 with best record	4	1
4 with worst record	0	4

Thus the instructors who had a higher trainee pass rate tended to be those who were trainee-oriented.

Many of the statements of the most successful instructors showed them to be especially perceptive of their trainee's reaction and their problems in learning. This question from the instructor with the highest pass rate of all suggests a man very much aware of how individual trainees feel:

'One man can master one thing and another can't. I speak to each trainee confidentially. I don't bring the other trainees in because I think this could bring discontent and there is always the trainee who might start to take things over saying, "this is the way to do it" ... It sometimes does hold the trainee back if he sees that the others are experienced men. I like to give him praise but I don't tell him he is good. It does depend a lot on the individual you have got. Usually by the second day you've got a pretty good idea of the character of the man and you know how far you can praise him and how far you can criticize him before he puts his foot down and says you're picking on him ... I usually have a chat with them at the start to let them know what I want from them and what they can expect from me. I like to get rid of any element of doubt in their minds. I'm inclined to give a bit of the official look in the beginning to create the impression that I am the instructor and they are the trainees. But as time goes on I do build up a bit of comradeship ... You've got to gain the man's confidence as well as give him confidence in himself. A man's got a terrific amount of concentration to give when he is in the cab and if he is concerned all the time that I am breathing down his neck it will be very unnerving.'

The following quotation comes from another instructor, who was amongst the least successful on pass rate:

'I can see the man who isn't going to make it in the period he's going to get ... it's a job that's got to be done and I do it to the best of my ability ... I look at a man and say: "he's going to make a driver". I look at another and know he's going to be a problem but they both get the same training as far as I'm concerned'.

Effects of previous education and work

The choice of instructor becomes crucial whenever individual trainees create special problems. But where those problems are shared by several trainees the situation is a little easier as firms come to recognize the significant effects of a common pattern of work experience and life style. Take the case of

miners. They have a reputation for exceeding expectations by
their performance in industry. Most of them have had to
adapt to continuous changes in technology over a long period
so that they make ready trainees. They carry with them the
sociability and sense of comradeship that have grown out of
the perils of the pit. They respond well to 'being treated right'
and if the initial hurdles are passed, become well integrated
into a new system. But the hurdles are distinctive and
peculiar. It may be something of a shock for the newly-fledged
personnel officer to be told by a miner that he is having difficulty in settling down 'because of the closed environment'!
Variants of this statement have been quoted many times
and in due course it becomes clear what is meant. The miner
may work in a narrow seam but he usually sees his supervisor
only once a shift. At other times he is free to move around as
he wishes. For him, it is being pinned down to a set work-
place that is the restriction. So his problems of learning may
centre not on acquiring work skill, not on fitting into the
working group, but on adjusting to those conditions of shop
floor discipline that conflict with that compensating freedom
so valued by men underground.

Other groups are distinctive because of the long-term effect
of their way of life. Former railway workers who in many
instances have worked in supervised gangs are easy to assimilate socially into the atmosphere of the factory. Housewives
returning to the work-force after their children have grown
up may, however, find the switch from the individualism of
maintaining a household to the socially compact atmosphere
of the factory a difficult one, and it is on the success or failure
of social assimilation that their re-entry to working life so
often rests.

With certain workers, the central problem is finding a way
of encouraging them to participate in learning. It mainly
occurs amongst those who have left school at an early age and
have pursued an unchanging traditional occupation over a
long period. One American study referred to the problems of
enrolling rural workers in further education and training.

Success was achieved when a training programme in agricultural mechanics was taken out into the fields, the only environmental context in which the workers were fully at ease. In another American study, workers in the steel industry boycotted or ignored opportunities for updating their technical knowledge by attendance at evening classes, even though such learning was crucial for holding on to their jobs and indispensable for promotion. But later, when their supervisors were trained to become their teachers, they responded to the opportunity and volunteered *en masse*, maintaining their numbers to the end of the course.

Retraining *within* the firm seems the one condition which compels or encourages companies to tailor their training plans to meet the collective problems of individuals with similar backgrounds. In most other cases, the skilful instructor is obliged to deal with individual problems as best he can, largely by adjusting the pace of a set programme and by pursuing questions and avenues of thought that are often idiosyncratic.

A readiness to cope with problems of individual differences becomes especially important in selecting applicants and in matching them to the jobs for which they are to receive training. The variations in ability that naturally exist between people are magnified by schooling and job history. So the level and depth of education and work-experience provide the main clues for assessment and guides to action.

Formal education has no bearing on the capacity to acquire high speed manual skills, but it has a most definite bearing on learning by understanding. The brawny labourers who were being trained as machine setters (*see* Chapter 2, Part 1) complained that they 'get so tired after this mental work'. As people age, lack of education and/or intelligence becomes an increasing handicap if there is a need to develop new concepts. But even a little education goes a long way. The boiler operators (*see* Chapter 6, Part 2) who had participated in *any* form of education or training since leaving school did better in their theoretical examinations than those who had not, even though they were no better in their practical work. Sometimes an establishment is well-known for the learning opportunities it provides and sometimes the converse is the case. One trainee over 40 years of age, on a steam-diesel conversion course, was performing poorly and his instructor remarked: 'He's been at a quiet depot where nothing changes much. They have gone on in the same way for years. So now he finds it difficult to pick up something new.' Others who did well were spoken of as 'coming from a good depot'.

A little *occupational* experience, like educational experience, can also go a long way. One study* of training in the clothing industry, showed that trainee machinists consistently had more than average difficulty in learning if they began training over the age of 25. Yet older women, in their mid-40s, with a year or so of teenage experience in machining and intervening decades of housework and childcare, often found themselves reaching experienced worker standards after a week or two of retraining. Sometimes the value of this remote experience is even more subtle. A few older women 'surprises' who have mastered fast and demanding jobs with remarkable facility have as their sole recommendation experience of a year or two on some unrelated piecework job during their youth. Many similar instances of what psychologists call transfer effects have been quoted to ITRU members by those concerned with personnel functions in industry. Amongst these are the allegations that shop assistants tend to make good machinists, that work study engineers make good foremen, that Merchant Marine officers make good work study managers, and that milkmen make good process workers in automated plants. Conversely, bus drivers are said to make poor postmen, and craftsmen to make poor training analysts. The claims tend to be followed by some sort of rationale. Milkmen are used to working abnormal hours, which process plants nearly always demand, and to working on their own which is often the requirement in a highly automated plant.

* *See* Belbin, E. and Sergean, R. *Training in the Clothing Industry.* London: Twentieth Century Press, 1963.

On the other hand bus drivers, while liking to get around, are spoilt by long experience of travel the (relatively) easy way and tend to be overconfident in their knowledge of local geography.

Spare-time interests

It would be difficult to check the validity of generalizations which are based on a few cases. But sometimes the importance of life experience comes through from methodical investigations. During the course of the work with London Transport, there was occasion to subject the trainee drivers to a large battery of selection tests. This included the Gibson Spiral Maze (a hand-eye co-ordination test), Raven's Matrices (an intelligence test), a verbal instructions test, the Eysenck Personality Inventory, and a biographical questionnaire. Not all the trainees took all the tests, but each test was completed by several hundred trainees. Yet all the tests proved poor indicators of ability to pass the bus driving examination. However, a questionnaire was later designed to pick up spare-time interests. From this it emerged that playing football was a better predictor of success than any of the tests! The predictions were better still when 'road experience' (none had direct experience of bus-driving and none held a full car licence) was taken into account. The trainees were allocated up to five points for experience based on (*a*) riding a bicycle in a town; (*b*) riding a motor bicycle; (*c*) driving a car; (*d*) tuition of ten hours or more in the last five years, anywhere; and (*e*) other vehicle experience anywhere. The first three categories were limited to experience in the British Isles, Australia, and Kenya. The applicant who had only 'driven' a rickshaw in Hong Kong earned one point under (*e*)! The overall results were as follows:

	Vehicle experience—cumulative points					
	0	1	2	3	4	5
Number of trainees	185	231	175	71	19	4
Per cent pass rate	12	25	46	56	68	100

It might seem a curious question to ask an applicant for a bus driver's job whether he played football or rode a bicycle but in fact it could be relevant. However it is not possible to assess the significance of this or any other items of previous experience without the systematic compilation of facts in a pilot study. The case for conducting such an investigation is strong wherever mature adults form an important part of the labour intake.

Older adults are likely to have had more experience than younger adults, so that the examination of their experience is far more rewarding, but we must be careful to separate what is meant by experience from the mere passage of time. Experience, according to Chambers dictionary, refers to *practical acquaintance with any matter gained by trial,* and there is no mention here of duration. Length of experience, which is what the man in the street often means by experience, has intrinsic value only where it encompasses variation and diversity. There is the oft-quoted story of the job applicant who claimed to have had ten years' experience of shop floor conditions. 'You mean one year's experience repeated ten times', retorted the personnel officer examining his record.

Nevertheless there is a sense in which duration of experience is relevant to performance. Repetitive situations produce repetitive responses which become crystallized into habits. The ex-regimental sergeant major, now a doorman and security guard, enacts his former role in his new job, even if his general stance and behaviour causes mirth when it is out of style with that of other employees in the organization. If an acquired habit is useful in an ostensibly different setting it is almost certain to appear. But acquired habits have also a way of intruding where they are not wanted. Then the individual will have to unlearn. This double imposition of needing to learn both what to do and what not to do seems to produce vastly greater difficulty than engaging in new learning on its own.

Those who work in training and personnel have a special responsibility for digging into and extracting the real nature

of personal experience. If this experience, with all its individual overtones, can be correctly interpreted there are good
prospects both of placing people in the right jobs and of
finding means of avoiding the tripwires along the path of
learning.

6. FOLLOWING-UP AFTER TRAINING

A careful induction of mature adults and a slow and careful
start to training do much to lay the seeds of success. But the
seeds do not always grow into plants that bear fruit. Success
in training is too readily taken to imply success in the job.
Ultimate progress depends on many factors. We were
taught this lesson by an early experience in our industrial
careers.

In the mid-1950s, a new method of training menders and
burlers (who invisibly rectify cloth) in the worsted industry
was set up in a centre established by the forerunner of the
Wool, Jute, and Flax Industry Training Board.* The scheme
was eventually adopted and employed throughout the
industry because of the consequent low failure rate and the
shortened period necessary to reach a given standard of skill.
Nevertheless, as on many highly skilled tasks, the individual
differences in competence were still quite large. It was not
unknown for the lowest third of the trainees to produce an
output around the target while the highest third sustained
an output 50 per cent higher. After the trainees dispersed to
their several firms, their output could be subsequently
measured, since all firms in the industry used the same yard-
stick of comparison. It was then noticed that there was virtu-
ally no association between individual productivity in the
training centre and individual productivity in the firm. Some
promising trainees fell back while others less promising made
steady progress. Further analysis emphasized the dominant
part played by the context of the firm which now over-

* See Belbin, E., Belbin, R. M., and Hill, F. 'A comparison between the
results of three different methods of operator training'. *Ergonomics*, 1, 39-50,
1957.

whelmed the individual differences previously noted. The standards set by management and the established practices of the working group both contribute to the norm to which the individual conforms.

The pressures of socialization in a given working environment produce a challenge to learning which is sometimes no less considerable than the challenge of learning a skill in a training centre. But whereas the younger trainee usually adjusts readily to what is expected, as in the worsted mills, the older trainee is more often liable to be disturbed by the change in demands and to react by leaving. An ITRU study of labour turnover* pointed to two critical periods of adjustment for older trainees, one on joining the training group and the other on transferring to the job. If these critical periods are passed, the older trainee has a much greater chance of survival on the job than the younger trainee.

What can be done then to ensure that the trainee survives the hurdles? One approach is a more persistent follow-up after the training to establish the factors that make for success.

A training department is usually tempted to choose recruits who are likely to perform well in training irrespective of other considerations. For example, some emerging information from several ITRU studies in selection suggests that intelligence (as measured by an intelligence test) correlates well with performance during the early stages of training but not during the later stages nor with subsequent productivity. High intelligence can be a strong qualification for a prospective trainee, but when eventually placed in a routine job, an intelligent trainee might prove a poor placement, often becoming bored with the job and losing interest. Another criterion commonly taken in acceptance for training is manual dexterity. Amongst thirty-five entrants to training for the job of weighing and packing fish in Mac Fisheries at Fraserburgh, there was a strong association between selection test score on a dexterity test and success in training. On the other

* *See* Newsham, D. B. *The Challenge of Change to the Adult Trainee.* Training Information Paper No. 3. London: HMSO, 1969.

hand, selection test score did not predict performance on the job after training. The explanation is probably that performance in training depends mainly on the acquisition of manual skill, while performance in production depends mainly on motivation. Many married women who return to the workforce for human company are less interested than others in reaching maximum bonus, but women who are saving up to get married are notably productive.

Since there are difficulties in training older workers (older meaning 'above the normal age of entry') it is natural that *trainability* should be given priority of consideration. But it is unfortunate if this means that *employability* is neglected. It is better to establish what employability means in a specific context in the first place. It might prove better in the long run to train people who are good employment prospects but none too easy to teach, than to take on those who are favourites for training but who are likely to make poor long-term prospects. Indeed, this is one of the advantages of recruiting mature adults. They may be more difficult to train but once established they prove stable and conscientious employees.

Lastly, following-up has another meaning but one which equally deserves attention. This is where the intention is to smooth the way, to cushion the impact of transition. Visits by someone from the training centre establish a bridge of continuity, reduce the sense of isolation and provide additional channels of communication. So a service is provided both to the trainees and to the department receiving them. The idiosyncrasies of trainees are often revealed in training and such information is ignored at peril. It was a catastrophe for Mrs. Chatton (*see* Chapter 3, Part 1), the oldest machinist her firm had ever trained, and it was a set-back for a brave experiment, when the job into which she was successfully introduced on the line suddenly changed to something physically similar but subjectively quite different. A training officer should have an intimate knowledge of those who pass through a training school and sense the way in which they will respond best to further development at work. If follow-up can be pursued in a diplomatic but purposive fashion, the chances of losing an investment in training will be much reduced.

8. Retraining and the Future

In the previous pages we have seen adult learners struggling, falling back, recovering, triumphing. Those who have won through have been upgraded, have found new occupational skills, or have adapted to new environments. If the focus of attention has centred on the successful or those who merely stumbled before rising, it is not due to a blindness to the frequency of failures, but to a belief that teachers in adult education and training can gain more by contemplating what is positive and what is possible.

The danger about recounting a few successful episodes in adult training is that achievement may appear all too easy and commonplace. There is a temptation in formulating future plans to suppose that the older learner is as well equipped as his younger counterpart—some would say better equipped—to progress in retraining. This sense of complacency—or optimism—may be founded on a blurring in the public mind between learning ability and *learned* ability. Many distinguished men, who have accumulated knowledge in their chosen fields of interest over many years, take pride in their ability to continue learning; but this does not mean that the man of letters who has previously been weak on mechanical matters is still capable of applying himself to the study of the internal combustion engine.

The difference between learning as a voluntary pastime and learning as a part of training can be compared with the difference between leisure and work. Both may provide opportunities for social relationships, invigorating exercise, and enjoyment. The essential difference is that, whatever the similarities in content, work involves an element of compulsion or obligation. Training, too, implies compulsion. You learn not what you wish but what you need and, indeed, must learn in order to become competent. The arbiter of these matters is not the learner but the teacher so that the conditions of training impose a degree of constraint and stress. It is this type of learning at which adults are much less adept and for which they are much less ready to present themselves.

It is timely to reflect on this problem when the country is on the verge of a massive expansion of facilities under the Training Opportunities Scheme and through the proposed establishment of a National Training Agency.

> '... The aim is to increase the capacity of the Government Training Centres and, in consultation with the interests concerned, to make more extensive use of training facilities in colleges of further education, employers' premises and other organisations so that 100,000 men and women a year can receive training under the scheme as soon as possible, and, as a first step, not less than 60-70,000 a year will get training by 1975...'*

Although the Government has emphasized that these proposals are not put forward as a panic measure in the face of a rise in unemployment to the million mark, most commentators have hailed the measures as a means of redeploying many of the unskilled men who have never had an opportunity in earlier years to learn a trade. Those who could benefit most by the proposals are the middle- and long-term unemployed who, as it happens, are over-represented in the higher age groups of the labour force. Will they seize the opportunity or will they too be reluctant learners?

The formal age limits to entry into Government-sponsored training centres in most countries of Western Europe were raised appreciably or removed altogether in the early 1960s, yet five years later Margaret Gordon observed: 'Few workers over about 45 years old have participated in these pro-

---

* *Training for the Future.* Published by HMSO for the Department of Employment, 1972.

grammes'.* Since then, the small numbers trained after the age of 40 have continued to arouse comment. The size of the task is evident from our book and the notice of it has not escaped the authors of *Training for the Future*:

> 'Careful attention will have to be given to marketing the new scheme. It is not enough to provide new opportunities; people must be told that they exist, and be convinced that training or retraining could offer real advantages to them personally'.

The prospects of turning bold plans into real achievement may depend on the intangible skills of those who administer and organize training rather than simply on the provision of facilities and the size of budgets. That is the message that can justifiably be extracted from the examples of the training of adults that have been collated in this book.

As society gains experience of retraining as a means of assisting people to move into new jobs, the more salient problems will in due course be uncovered. In previous chapters we have attempted to intimate their nature in advance of the experience which the national effort will provide. So we may conclude in our last few pages by re-asking the questions that each chapter has suggested, while we continue through research to seek more refined answers and new and imaginative approaches.

* Gordon, Margaret S. *Retraining and Labor Market Adjustment in Western Europe*. Manpower Automation Research Monograph No. 4. Washington: U.S. Department of Labor, 1965.

SOME PROBLEMS IN THE RECRUITMENT AND TRAINING OF ADULTS

The questions relate to the subject matter of Chapters 1 to 6.

Chapter 1

1. How do the following groups differ in the way they react to or take advantage of new and unfamiliar job opportunities: younger and older workers; men and women; those in the process of changing jobs and those attempting to emerge from a period of unemployment or (in the case of women) domesticity?

2. How will these groups respond to the first impression that a firm creates?

3. How can induction procedures be developed to take into account the needs of each group?

4. How can firms best attract those who have never had an industrial skill without introducing a note of condescension?

5. What techniques introduce a personal touch into the recruitment and placement of older applicants?

6. How can the need to recruit suitable personnel be reconciled with the need to allay the fears that many applicants suffer in rigorous selection procedures?

7. The characteristics of those selected can be studied, but what clues are there on the job capabilities of others who might prove suitable but who are not usually considered, or those who would be reluctant to apply?

Chapter 2

8. How can one distinguish between facilitating anxiety and disruptive anxiety?

9. What is the significance of this distinction for training?

10. Why is disruptive anxiety more commonly found amongst older trainees than amongst younger?

11. What steps can be taken in planning a training programme to remove the most likely causes of tension?
12. How can one establish whether a display of nervousness is merely a symptom of some deficiency that the trainee is trying to hide?
13. Which is better: to begin training and attempt to dispel anxiety as the course proceeds, or to postpone the start until everyone is at ease?

Chapter 3

14. What jobs would be especially difficult for the late starter?
15. Is there any empirical evidence about the age at which difficulties in learning begin to become apparent in particular operations?
16. Can the nature of the difficulties which older trainees experience be identified?
17. Could these be overcome by changes in the method of training?
18. Why could it be useful to analyse the difficulties of older learners even if the bulk of the intake were young?
19. What factors lie behind the tendency for people to avoid learning the things that most others have learnt earlier in life?
20. How can older learners best be weaned away from hard-and-fast attitudes that have developed over a long period?

Chapter 4

21. Does a good start in training indicate high potential capacity for the job?
22. Correspondingly, does a poor start indicate low capacity?
23. How can one distinguish between lack of aptitude in a trainee and the consequences of some peripheral difficulty?
24. What are the factors that commonly account for a slow start?

25. How do these factors change in their order of importance as trainees increase in age?
26. What factors are capable of triggering off a leap forward in learning?

Chapter 5

27. What inherent advantages can four-hour twilight shifts offer for older starters?
28. What social and environmental conditions are most conducive to progress in adult training?
29. What can the training officer do to further good social relationships?
30. How do older and poorly educated trainees differ from others in the nature of the help they need from training officers?
31. How best can the need for technical progress in training be reconciled with the cultivation of a spirit of adventure, development, and personal fulfilment amongst trainees?

Chapter 6

32. Are there areas of learning in which people could progress well on their own without continuous surveillance and direction by instructors?
33. When and where should instructors intercede, and when and where should they limit their role?
34. How can the capacity for self-organization and self-help best be developed in trainees?
35. To what extent can self-help and self-development contribute to the removal of psychological barriers to technical change?
36. How best can teachers be taught to combine insistence on high standards with the involvement of trainees in decision-making?

General Questions

37. What are the special qualities needed in those who teach adults?
38. What are the implications of the content of this book for the training of instructors?
39. Which types of occupational skill are most suitable for an older working population facing redeployment and retraining?
40. What steps can be taken to encourage middle-aged adults who are reluctant to leave home to enter residential training centres?
41. Under what circumstances is it better to take training to people rather than to expect them to disperse to training centres where the courses they seek are on offer?
42. What advantages can be built into mobile training facilities to compensate for their intrinsic limitations?
43. How can the technology of training best be harnessed to meet the highly individual needs of adult trainees?

Index